If I Could Ask God *One* Question . . .

If I Could Ask God One Question...

GREG JOHNSON

Illustrated by Steve Bjorkman

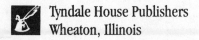
Tyndale House Publishers
Wheaton, Illinois

Library of Congress Cataloging-in-Publication Data

Johnson, Greg, date
    If I could ask God one question— / Greg Johnson
      p.   cm.
    Summary: Provides biblically based answers to the most commonly
asked questions about God and the Christian faith.
    ISBN 0-8423-1616-7 (pbk.)
    1. Teenagers—Religious life—Miscellanea. 2. Theology,
Doctrinal—Popular works. 3. Christian life—Juvenile literature.
[1. Christian life. 2. Questions and answers.] I. Title.
BV4531.2.J58   1991
248.8'3—dc20   91-65304

Printed in the United States of America

99 98 97 96 95 94 93 92 91
10 9   8   7   6   5   4   3   2

To my two sons, Troy *and* Drew. *May you never fear asking the right questions and never tire of seeking the right answers.*

To the men and women in youth work, who give their lives away to teens every day. There are very few things more important than what you do.

Introduction

As a Christian of seventeen years, I've never been afraid to ask God the tough questions. I've always been the type who had to know. Thankfully, the people who pointed me to Christ consistently led me to the Bible for the answers I sought.

Typically, I asked a lot of irrelevant questions the Bible never intended to answer. But for 95 percent of the *important* questions I asked, God's Word was always there, ready and waiting to give me the truth. The other 5 percent? I'll have to wait for heaven . . . in this life, they're unanswerable. That's okay.

Perhaps you're a brand-new Christian who's starting from scratch. The Bible looks like a big book with no pictures, and living the Christian life is . . . well . . . something too confusing to think about. This book is for you.

Or maybe you've grown up in the church and suddenly are asking the whys and hows to a faith that's becoming your own and is a little tougher to grow into. The Scriptures and illustrations used will hopefully cause *your faith* to be brought into clearer focus.

Either way, for as long as you live, God's not intimidated by *anything*—least of all, honest feelings and questions asked from a heart genuinely looking for an answer. Since we can't intimidate or surprise him, maybe we should try to please him!

What God enjoys most is progress. When you move from point A to point B, as you're heading to point Z, you've made progress.

The pages following are designed to aid in your progress toward the goal of understanding the Bible and loving God with all your heart, your soul, and your mind.

The questions and answers in this book have come from two sources: thirteen years of working with teenagers, and the Bible. Though some of the questions are tough, the answers are simple.

Being a Christian wasn't intended to be a *religion* that only a few could figure out, but a *relationship* based on trust. Though Jesus loves the intellectual who "has to know," he especially delights in believers who simply want to be with him. As you seek the answers to your questions, realize this: There's no greater joy than simply being with Jesus the Christ and allowing his Word to remind you that he loves you deeply, each new day.

"Do as they say," the Lord replied, *"for I am the one they are rejecting, not you—they don't want me to be their king any longer."* 1 Samuel 8:7

So many things try to crowd God out of my life. How much of me does God want?

The answer is, he wants all of you. God does not want to be just another addition to your life—he wants everything you do to revolve around him!

Bike tires are only as strong as the hub of the wheel. If a tire was made up only of rim and spokes, the wheel would soon collapse under the constant pounding and pressure.

The spokes in our lives are those things that are important to us, like family, friends, school, sports, or entertainment. If our life revolves around any one of these "spokes," eventually the constant pounding and pressures of our world will wear us down and possibly cause us to collapse.

God knows this and has provided the strong center that will hold us together. By ignoring God and trying to run our own lives, we will be living as though we believe the spokes are strong enough to carry us.

For centuries the Jewish people complained to God and asked him for a king to rule over them. What they were actually saying was, "God, since we cannot see you, we cannot trust you to take care of us. Give us someone we can see who will rule over us." Eventually God gave in to their request. The results however were devastating. Because they put their focus on what a man could do for them (a weak "spoke"), their enemies soon overpowered the entire nation until all of the people of Israel were forced to live away from the Promised Land.

The Old Testament graphically describes what happened when God's people rejected him from being their leader (the hub).

Jesus Christ should be the hub of our lives. This means that we should consult him and his Word first.

When things begin to crowd out your relationship with God, try writing down all of your "priorities." Ask a trusted Christian friend if any one of these "spokes" is taking the place of God in your life.

For I know the plans I have for you, says the Lord. They are plans for good and not for evil, to give you a future and a hope. In those days when you pray, I will listen. You will find me when you seek me, if you look for me in earnest. Jeremiah 29:11-13

I'm afraid to give my whole life to God. I'm thinking that he's going to ask me to do things later on, like be a missionary in another country. I really don't want to do that. What happens if I hold back part of my life from God?

Imagine going out for basketball and telling the coach that you only want to practice, not play in the games. Or that you only want to play in the first half of each game. How would your coach react? What would your teammates say?

Undoubtedly they would be a little upset at your selfish attitude. After all, if you're going to be on the team, you should play in the games. And if you play, you shouldn't avoid the last half when your team might need you the most. Besides, playing the game is a lot better than practice. And the second half is when the game is on the line.

Unfortunately, many Christians by their attitudes and their actions tell the coach (God) two things: they don't really want the benefits and the fun of playing on the team (besides heaven, of course); and they don't want to contribute during the times when other people might need them the most.

God wants your whole life, so he can make something extraordinary out of it. Jesus told his followers, "The thief's purpose is to steal, kill and destroy. My purpose is to give life in all its fullness" (John 10:10). That's a level of trust you haven't reached yet.

The Christian life was never meant to be done halfway. Some would say you can't do it halfway at all. You're either sold out to God or sold out to the world.

For God to give you "life in all its fullness," you must give your full life to God. Jesus said, "If you cling to your life, you will lose it; but if you give it up for me, you will save it" (Matthew 10:39).

If God asks you to be a missionary to another country, in effect he is saying, "I know you better than anyone else does. I made you, and I love you more than you'll ever know. Because I put you together, I know what it will take to make you the happiest and most fulfilled in life. If you choose any other direction, you'll be settling for second best. Please don't."

God's goal isn't to make his kids miserable; he wants to lead us in a direction that will cause us to say, "The game wasn't easy, God, especially the last quarter. Thanks for believing in me enough to put me in. I really had fun."

Now change your mind and attitude to God and turn to him so he can cleanse away your sins and send you wonderful times of refreshment from the presence of the Lord. Acts 3:19

My mom has said some pretty bad things to me over the years. Now that I'm a Christian, I know I should forgive her, but I can't. What should I do?

The gap between knowing you need to forgive someone and actually being able to do it can seem like a vast canyon. You can see the other side, but getting there seems impossible.

Remember when the shower drain was plugged up with a two-month accumulation of hair? The water would only slowly seep through the greasy, soapy mass. Rarely will a plunger work on gross buildups of stuff in the drain. No amount of suction trying to bring the glob up is strong enough, because the clog is too deep.

The next approach usually is to burn away the clog by applying something like Drāno. Sometimes this will work if the buildup is not too severe. The last resort, of course, is to call a plumber. He'll come in with a narrow, hard, and flexible piece of metal called a "snake" and drill right through the clog until the water is flowing freely.

Unforgiveness is like a clogged drain. Sometimes it is fairly easy to unclog. People hurt us, we let them know they hurt us, they say they're sorry, we forgive them, and the whole episode is usually forgotten.

Unforgiveness from hurts over a number of years is what a drain would look like after years of giving your dog a bath in the sink and never cleaning it. You might as well buy a new sink.

Although it is gross to think about, our sin is like a huge hair ball clogging our relationship with God. Until it is removed, we can never really receive anything meaningful from him. Jesus came to unclog our "pipe" so God's love and forgiveness could flow through to us. Though he did nothing wrong, he had to die to do it.

Your mom's sin against you has clogged your relationship. Although you may have done nothing wrong, you must "die" in a sense, so that your relationship can be clean again. Otherwise the clog will only get worse.

You may have every right not to forgive your mom; but you must put aside that right for a greater goal—learning how you and your mom can love each other.

God took the initiative with us by humbling himself and forgiving all of our sin (to see the comparison of how much God has forgiven us and how much we must forgive others, see Matthew 18:21-34). You must do the same with the person who has wronged you.

The forgiveness must be from your heart and must not be dependent upon whether she feels sorry for what she has done. Forgiving someone is a gift only you can offer. You can't make people take a free gift—they must reach out and receive it. Though the canyon looks deep and treacherous, the reward on the other side is a clear conscience and, you hope, a renewed relationship.

And now just as you trusted Christ to save you, trust him, too, for each day's problems; live in vital union with him. Let your roots grow down into him and draw up nourishment from him.
Colossians 2:6-7

I've been a Christian for about two months and I feel so far behind spiritually, especially compared to friends who have been Christians for a lot longer. Sometimes it gets pretty discouraging. How do I catch up?

We live in a world that makes it nearly impossible not to compare ourselves with others. Whether it's looks, clothes, athletic abilities, or other talents, it seems everyone's goal is to be up to, or beyond, someone else's level.

Sometimes we even compare our life as a Christian to others'. You must, however, fight this urge and recognize two essential facts.

First, receiving forgiveness for our sin and asking Christ to come into our life is like having a seed planted in our heart (see 1 Corinthians 3:6). Any seed planted must first take root before it grows and blossoms.

Do you remember in first grade when you planted a seed in a clear plastic cup? If the seed was planted close enough to the edge, you would see that the roots would grow downward first; then a few days later a plant would appear above the dirt. It was miraculous!

The only difference between you and your friends is that they have had more time to spread their roots down deep. They've lived longer in "vital union with him" and have "drawn up nourishment from him" for a longer period of time.

When you took the first step of faith to trust Christ with your life, that was like the seed being planted. From this point it's up to *you* and *God* to nourish the seed.

Your faith is nourished by rooting your new relationship with Christ. This means getting to know God better through reading and obeying his Word—the Bible (Romans 10:17). As with any relationship, time together helps you to appreciate God's character and

7

will lead to a greater love for him (2 Peter 3:18).

Second, God doesn't compare one Christian to another. So don't you try. That would be like a father wanting his two-year-old son to throw a baseball as well as his nine-year-old. He can't.

As Christians, we never get to a point where we have arrived and are totally mature. Our love and appreciation for God can always grow deeper as he shows us new areas in our lives to trust him with.

Enjoy these beginning stages of your faith by taking in all of the spiritual nourishment you can handle. Remember, the stronger and deeper your roots grow below the surface, the more beautiful and fruitful you will be as a Christian (see John 15:4-5).

Jesus' disciples saw him do many other miracles besides the ones told about in this book, but these are recorded so that you will believe that he is the Messiah, the Son of God, and that believing in him you will have life. John 20:30-31

After I became a Christian I was told to start reading the Bible. But it's hard to understand and is bigger than any book I ever even attempted to read. Where do I start?

Unfortunately, no place in the Bible does it say, "Start here," and then, "Read this next." So, we need help.

When two people in love have to be separated for a while, they usually send streams of letters to each other. Webbed inside the boring facts about daily life is a story of love and devotion to the other person.

To find the "good stuff" you would have to wade through the details. If you wanted to find out how the relationship developed, you would need to study the details.

Sometimes that's how it is with the Bible. The events that occurred so long ago don't seem to have any relevance to us today. But if your goal is to understand the relationship between God and his people, from Adam to Jesus, those details become essential information.

New Christians usually want the "good stuff." Later, as they grow in their faith, they'll be more interested in the details that will help them put God's whole plan together.

So for now, consider these suggestions.

- Get to know Jesus the Christ. Listen to his words. Try to understand what each story is saying and watch how Christ treats others. John tells us that he wrote his book "so that you will believe that [Jesus] is the Messiah, the Son of God, and that believing in him you will have life" (John 20:31). The first four books of the New Testament give four different perspectives on Jesus' life. Getting to know him should be your first priority.

- Next, start reading through some of the smaller letters that Paul, Peter, and John wrote (Paul's letters are everything from Romans to Philemon).

- Try Proverbs next. You can read one chapter a day and finish the book in a month.
- After this, read Genesis, Exodus, Daniel, and Jonah. They offer stories of real people whose problems were not all that different from yours. Learn from their lives so that you don't make the same mistakes they did.

There's no shortcut to the Christian life. We must be disciplined enough to dig in the Bible to find all the buried treasure that God wants to give those who will dig deep enough. Have fun!

I don't understand myself at all, for I really want to do what is right, but I can't. I do what I don't want to—what I hate. I know perfectly well that what I am doing is wrong, and my bad conscience proves that I agree with these laws I am breaking. But I can't help myself because I'm no longer doing it. It is sin inside me that is stronger than I am that makes me do these evil things.

I know I am rotten through and through so far as my old sinful nature is concerned. No matter which way I turn I can't make myself do right. I want to but I can't. When I want to do good, I don't; and when I try not to do wrong, I do it anyway. Now if I am doing what I don't want to, it is plain where the trouble is; sin still has me in its evil grasp.

It seems to be a fact of life that when I want to do what is right, I inevitably do what is wrong. . . .

So there is now no condemnation awaiting those who belong to Christ Jesus. For the power of the life-giving Spirit—and this power is mine through Christ Jesus—has freed me from the vicious circle of sin and death. Romans 7:15-21; 8:1-2

Since becoming a Christian, it seems like I'm always fighting against certain thoughts and habits that I used to never give a second thought about.

Picture your life as a door. Before you became a Christian, your sins were like nails pounded into the door and left there. When you asked Christ to forgive you, all of the nails you'd collected were removed. Unfortunately, what was left was a door full of holes, not very pleasant to look at and not very useful.

But God began patching up the holes. More accurately, he began to heal the scars left by sin, so the door looked unscarred even after years of constant pounding. We can truly become a new creation (see 2 Corinthians 5:17).

That's why it's so important for people to come to know Christ's forgiveness early in life. Because we inherited a sinful nature from Adam (Romans 5:12), time and wrong choices can pound some pretty large nails into our lives. And those scars may take longer to heal.

What you're experiencing is a new sensitivity to sin. Since sin wants to "drive a hole" in you, and Christ wants to keep you unscarred by the effects of sin, it's no longer comfortable to ignore the constant pounding. Confessing your sin will always remove the nail.

This new sensitivity to sin means two things.

First, it's a definite sign that God's Holy Spirit has truly entered your life (Romans 8:9). It's likely you would still be numb to the nails (sin) if you had rejected Christ's forgiveness.

Second, it means that God is reminding you of his great love for you (Romans 8:38-39). Now your conscience advises you where you could stray off course. God does not want you to be left scarred by the consequences of your sin, so he begins at the source of it—your thought life.

Yet it was our *grief he bore,* our *sorrows that weighed him down. And we thought his troubles were a punishment from God, for his* own *sins! But he was wounded and bruised for* our *sins. He was beaten that we might have peace; he was lashed—and we were healed!* We—*every one of us—have strayed away like sheep!* We, *who left God's paths to follow our own. Yet God laid on* him *the guilt and sins of every one of us!* . . . *He was buried like a criminal, but in a rich man's grave; but he had done no wrong and had never spoken an evil word.* . . . *Therefore, I will give him the honors of one who is mighty and great because he has poured out his soul unto death. He was counted as a sinner, and he bore the sins of many, and he pled with God for sinners.*
Isaiah 53:4-6, 9, 12

I'm trying to understand how the Old Testament and the New Testament relate to each other. Which one is more important?

It's not that one is more important than the other. Instead it's a question of timing.

Imagine being seven years old and your parents sitting you down and telling you all of the rules about driving a car. Not only would you tune them out after about two minutes, but ten years later, when it came time to drive, you wouldn't remember anything they said.

Timing is everything. Wise parents have figured this out; that's why they didn't give you all the house rules as soon as you could talk. They waited until you were ready so that you would *want to listen,* you would *understand the rules,* and you would *remember what they said.*

The Old Testament was given to us for several reasons. After explaining creation, the main purpose of it was to point the way to God's solution for the problem of man's sin.

Romans 7:7 tells us that the Old Testament law was good because it showed us what sin was and thus showed us our need for a Savior.

The Old Testament points directly to Christ as the Savior that we needed. There are dozens of verses that tell the exact place of Jesus' birth, his sinless life, his death on a cross, his resurrection, and his return. Though it was written from about 1450–400 B.C., it predicts minute details about the life of Jesus. This also serves to prove the authority of the Scriptures.

Finally, the Old Testament helps the New Testament make sense. A few examples are found in this passage from Isaiah. To take away sin, the Hebrews had to sacrifice a lamb at a festival called "Passover." When Christ was sacrificed on the Cross, it showed how God had been "setting up" the world. Passover had been just a symbol of what Christ was to do on the Cross. For centuries the Hebrews had made yearly sacrifices to take away sin and guilt. In Christ, only one sacrifice was needed.

O loving and kind God, have mercy. Have pity upon me and take away the awful stain of my transgressions. Oh, wash me, cleanse me from this guilt. Let me be pure again. For I admit my shameful deed—it haunts me day and night. It is against you and you alone I sinned and did this terrible thing. You saw it all, and your sentence against me is just. But I was born a sinner, yes, from the moment my mother conceived me. You deserve honesty from the heart; yes, utter sincerity and truthfulness. Oh, give me this wisdom.

Sprinkle me with the cleansing blood and I shall be clean again. Wash me and I shall be whiter than snow. And after you have punished me, give me back my joy again. Don't keep looking at my sins—erase them from your sight. Create in me a new, clean heart, O God, filled with clean thoughts and right desires. Don't toss me aside, banished forever from your presence. Don't take your Holy Spirit from me. Restore to me again the joy of your salvation, and make me willing to obey you. Then I will teach your ways to other sinners, and they—guilty like me—will repent and return to you. Don't sentence me to death. O my God, you alone can rescue me. Then I will sing of your forgiveness, for my lips will be unsealed—oh, how I will praise you. Psalm 51:1-15

I heard something about a sin that God cannot forgive. What is it?

What you are referring to is sinning against the Holy Spirit. "Even blasphemy against me or any other sin, can be forgiven—all except one: speaking against the Holy Spirit shall never be forgiven, either in this world or in the world to come" (Matthew 12:31-32).

As you read in this Psalm, everyone is born a sinner (51:5). Left to ourselves, we would certainly die, because our sinful nature separates us from God and from real *life* (Romans 3:23; 6:23).

The good news is God didn't leave us on our own. He sent Jesus to pay our penalty and to die in our place. This way he killed sin forever. All who receive Christ into their life and accept his gift of forgiveness are forgiven—period (John 1:12).

The only sinner that can't be forgiven is someone who refuses to receive Christ, ignoring or rejecting the Holy Spirit's work in his or her life.

The incident that caused King David to pray the prayer in Psalm 51 is found in 2 Samuel 12:1-23. David not only committed adultery, but he had the woman's husband murdered so he could marry her. That's pretty bad behavior for a king.

When confronted with his sin a year after those events, David repented. He asked God to forgive him and renew their relationship once again.

Though David's sins were great, God forgave him. God is always willing to forgive those who admit their mistakes and who genuinely try not to repeat them.

It has been said that "the only sin God cannot forgive is the one we have not confessed."

By daily coming to God in humility, trust, and dependence, we show him that we mean business in keeping our relationship with him clean and growing.

David's prayer is the perfect example of a humble heart seeking after the only thing in life that really matters—a close relationship with God.

In response to all he has done for us, let us outdo each other in being helpful and kind to each other and in doing good. Let us not neglect our church meetings, as some people do, but encourage and warn each other, especially now that the day of his coming back again is drawing near. Hebrews 10:24-25

I like the idea about having a personal faith in God. What I don't like is having to go to church. It seems boring and a waste of time. I've been to a lot of churches and it all seems the same. Why can't there be a church with just kids my own age?

Imagine growing up without a family. It's tough to think of life without at least one parent who really cares.

Now imagine growing up with just brothers and sisters in the house and no parents at all. For a day or two it may seem like heaven, but very soon you would see that it's chaos. Eventually you'd miss having someone to take care of your basic needs.

Families are designed to take care of your daily needs and to give you the continual love and guidance you need as you're growing up. Because Mom and Dad have been around longer, they often know what to do when a tough circumstance comes up (as much as you may hate to admit it).

Jude 21 says to "stay always within the boundaries where God's love can reach and bless you."

Church is our spiritual family. If we stay away, we're left to try to survive by ourselves. If all we had around were other kids, church would be like a house with no adults. Pretty soon we'd recognize that many of our needs were not getting met.

The church, like the family, can often be under-appreciated for the role it plays in our spiritual growth. Some Christians don't recognize its influence until years later, when they realize they'd still be spiritual babies without the church's influence and love.

Then Jesus went out to the seashore again and preached to the crowds that gathered around him. As he was walking up the beach he saw Levi, the son of Alphaeus, sitting at his tax collection booth. "Come with me," Jesus told him. "Come be my disciple."

And Levi jumped to his feet and went along.

That night Levi invited his fellow tax collectors and many other notorious sinners to be his dinner guests so that they could meet Jesus and his disciples. (There were many men of this type among the crowds that followed him.) But when some of the Jewish religious leaders saw him eating with these men of ill repute, they said to his disciples, "How can he stand it, to eat with such scum?"

When Jesus heard what they were saying, he told them, "Sick people need the doctor, not healthy ones! I haven't come to tell good people to repent, but the bad ones." Mark 2:13-17

I used to like to go to parties a lot before I became a Christian. Are parties bad?

In answering this type of question, it's tough not to sound heavy-handed. After all, teenage parties do not exactly have a great reputation.

The key word to remember is not *yes* or *no* but *why?*—your motive is the key.

If you're honest, you'll have to agree that many of the reasons people party are pretty selfish. *Most* parties cater to the notion that it's a person's right to have a good time, especially if it's not hurting anyone else.

If someone is living apart from God, why would he or she think anything different? The Bible agrees that if this life doesn't matter, then "eat, drink and be merry. What's the difference? For tomorrow we die, and that ends everything!" (1 Corinthians 15:32).

The motive behind going to parties is what God is most concerned about. If it's to get drunk, take drugs, pick up the opposite sex, then

18

God wouldn't want you at parties.

The motive might be to be seen with the "cool" people. Being with certain people sometimes may help you feel accepted and even popular. But God accepts you as you are, and his acceptance is more important than anyone else's.

Jesus isn't against parties. He went to parties, and was, in fact, the life of the party! But his motives were entirely different from the selfish ones described above. He went to show people that he accepted them, to communicate truth about the character of God, and to celebrate life.

Should you do the same?

Perhaps, but here are a few questions you should consider:

- Have you grown sufficiently in your faith that you'll not be tempted if there's pressure to drink (or whatever)?
- Do you know someone who'll go with so you can encourage each other to stay clean?
- Are you going as a light or a hammer? That is, do you genuinely want to help those in darkness, or do you want to pound on others to justify your own "moral" life-style?
- Is there a chance that you could be found "guilty by association"? When others hear you were at the party, how will they know you didn't drink? Is it worth the hassle it may cause in making sure your reputation stays intact?
- What do your parents think about your attending that party? Would you have to *not tell them* in order to go?

Remember, although motive is the key, even the results of good motives may be more than you can handle.

Then he [Jesus] told this story to some who boasted of their virtue and scorned everyone else:

"Two men went to the Temple to pray. One was a proud, self-righteous Pharisee, and the other a cheating tax collector. The proud Pharisee 'prayed' this prayer: 'Thank God, I am not a sinner like everyone else, especially like that tax collector over there! For I never cheat, I don't commit adultery, I go without food twice a week, and I give to God a tenth of everything I earn.'

"But the corrupt tax collector stood at a distance and dared not even lift his eyes to heaven as he prayed, but beat upon his chest in sorrow, exclaiming, 'God, be merciful to me, a sinner.' I tell you, this sinner, not the Pharisee, returned home forgiven! For the proud shall be humbled, but the humble shall be honored." Luke 18:9-14

I've always been taught to be independent and self-sufficient. My youth leader says this isn't right. What's wrong with being proud about doing your best?

Have you ever known someone who thought they were so good in sports that they rarely listened to the coach? Although all coaches love to have players with great natural ability, most would settle for those with a few skills who are teachable. An athlete is much easier to mold than to push.

A totally self-reliant person is sort of like an athlete who allows the coach to give him advice *only when he or she wants it.* Before too long the athlete will start to deteriorate, in talent *and* in the eyes of the coach. In the same way, we need to depend on God to lead us. And we should do what he says.

God wants us always to try to do our best. We should never do anything halfway. But there's a difference between doing our best and allowing God to do his best through us.

Taking the credit for everything we do is called pride—it's a dangerous attitude.

There's a good type of pride that comes from doing something well. Perhaps we've worked hard, worked through some problems, and everything has come out great. We feel good about ourselves. The problem comes when we take the credit. That's the wrong kind of pride.

God wants us to recognize that he gave us our life and our talents. When we do, it shows humility and a deep respect for him.

The Pharisee in Luke 18 is a perfect example of someone with "bad pride." He was proud of his "holy" life. Although he acted like he was talking to God, he was really just talking to himself.

On the flip side is the tax collector. He had nothing to be proud of, especially in his relationship with God. In humility, he asked God for mercy.

If we go through life with an I-can-make-it-okay-by-myself attitude, we're really saying to God, "I don't really need you after all."

Then we will no longer be like children, forever changing our minds about what we believe because someone has told us something different or has cleverly lied to us and made the lie sound like the truth. Instead, we will lovingly follow the truth at all times—speaking truly, dealing truly, living truly.
Ephesians 4:14-15

What does it mean to "grow as a Christian"?

Spiritual growth is a lot like physical growth. In order to stay healthy and grow physically, we must eat the right foods, exercise, and get plenty of rest. You've heard that since you were a child. To grow spiritually involves the same formula.

Eating the right foods, as a Christian, means consuming the right spiritual "food." Many Christians are trying to survive on "fast food." That is, they watch Christian TV, read Christian magazines, and listen to Christian music, but they rarely give attention to God's Word.

There's only one food that will nourish our souls—the Bible. Everything else is only meant to be supplementary.

Exercise, as a Christian, involves resisting temptations, enduring trials, serving others, and telling others about our faith.

We need to be pushed in order to stay strong. This means exercise. Temptation and problems test our character; serving others stretches our faith; telling people about Christ strengthens our devotion.

Rest for the Christian is worship. Our world has a tendency to tighten us, like a rubber band pulled to the limit. Unless we take time weekly (and daily!) to recognize and worship God, he won't have the opportunity to minister to our needs.

We need sleep, rest, and times of vacation in order to get our physical batteries recharged. And we need worship to keep us spiritually renewed.

Growth takes time—a lifetime! And this means growing in a relationship, not just changing our behavior.

The Christian life is learning how to love the person of Jesus Christ more each day, staying close to him, and getting to know him better.

And now, dear brothers, I want you to know what happens to a Christian when he dies so that when it happens, you will not be full of sorrow, as those are who have no hope. For since we believe that Jesus died and then came back to life again, we can also believe that when Jesus returns, God will bring back with him all the Christians who have died. 1 Thessalonians 4:13-14

Even though I know I'm going to heaven, I'm still afraid of dying. How can I quit being so afraid of death?

Extreme fear of the unknown can cripple a person. Unfortunately, death is an unknown for everyone, even for Christians.

What will we find on the other side? How is God going to take me? Will the people left behind be able to adjust? What if I die before I have a chance to get married or see some places I want to see?

There are some questions without concrete answers. And that can be frustrating.

Someone once said that trying to explain to another person what God and heaven are like is like a dog telling another dog what it's like to be a human. It's impossible!

But death is not something that Christians have to fear.

Death, for the Christian, isn't the end of the story. It's the gateway to a place of indescribable joy and beauty. It's the beginning of a new life!

Fear is a learned emotion. Through the years we're conditioned to fear certain things. Little kids aren't afraid of death because they don't understand it. Yet as they grow and see the response of adults and the media to death, they learn that it's something awful and to be avoided at all cost.

After we become Christians, often we need to go through a relearning process about death. Paul, the author of half the New Testament, said this about death: "For to me, living means opportunities for Christ, and dying—well, that's better yet!" (Philippians 1:21).

Paul had learned that death would actually put an end to the struggles he faced on earth. He looked forward to the day when he could see Christ face to face. In the meantime, though, he had work to do—win people to Christ. Life wasn't a chore—it was a privilege!

Fear of dying doesn't disappear instantly. But as you spend time in the Bible and with other Christians who have the same hope as you do, you'll grow to realize that death is only a door to an eternity far better than your wildest dreams.

"Will a man rob God? Surely not! And yet you have robbed me.
  "'What do you mean? When did we ever rob you?'
  "You have robbed me of the tithes and offerings due to me. And
so the awesome curse of God is cursing you, for your whole
nation has been robbing me. Bring all the tithes into the
storehouse so that there will be food enough in my Temple; if you
do, I will open up the windows of heaven for you and pour out a
blessing so great you won't have room enough to take it in!"
Malachi 3:8-10

I see the offering plate passed every Sunday. I'm only a kid. Am I supposed to be giving my money to the church?

Jesus talked about money more than he talked about anything else. That's because money, more than any other possession, can take a strong foothold in our life. It can even control us.

Money by itself, of course, isn't evil. But the love of money leads to all sorts of problems (see 1 Timothy 6:10).

Though not loaded with money, young people almost always have cash to spend from part-time jobs, gifts, and allowances.

If you were to keep track of where your money goes, you probably would find that you spend it on clothes, music, junk food, perhaps gas for the car (if you drive), and, once in a while, gifts for others. Most of your money you spend on yourself.

God doesn't want *anything* to take his place in our life. For many, money often becomes their god (especially those who don't know Christ).

The best way to keep from making money our god is to learn the joy of giving it away. Building this habit must begin when you're young.

God doesn't need our money. He already owns everything! But *we* have a need to give it away. It's an incredible feeling to see our money go for something besides ourselves.

Here's a suggestion on how to start giving your money back to God. Each time you get some (whether through employment, allowance, or gift), take 10 percent out and put it in an envelope that says JESUS on it. It doesn't matter if it's fifty cents from a five dollar allowance or ten dollars from a hundred-dollar paycheck. Collect it for a month.

Next, decide to what or to whom you want to give it. Most churches have missionaries they support (people who have given their lives to spread the Good News of Jesus Christ). Select a missionary and ask to receive his or her monthly prayer letter. By giving to a missionary (even if it's $7.23 a month!), you're furthering the cause of Christ here on earth—and you're making a wise investment in others' eternity!

Or you might want to support a child overseas who needs the basics to survive. There are several good organizations that will give you the name of a needy child you can help support, usually for about twenty dollars per month. This may be a larger investment than you want to make, but the fun of knowing you're helping a "real person" is worth it!

Of course, you can also give it directly to your church in the offering plate and let them decide on how to use it.

At first, it may hurt a little, seeing your money go to something besides yourself. Eventually, however, you'll find you're having such a good time giving that you will want to give more!

Remember, it doesn't matter how much you give. It only matters that you give what you can. See Luke 21:1-4 for a good illustration of this point.

So they seized him and led him to the High Priest's residence, and Peter followed at a distance. The soldiers lit a fire in the courtyard and sat around it for warmth, and Peter joined them there.

A servant girl noticed him in the firelight and began staring at him. Finally she spoke: "This man was with Jesus!"

Peter denied it. "Woman," he said, "I don't even know the man!"

After a while someone else looked at him and said, "You must be one of them!"

"No sir, I am not!" Peter replied.

About an hour later someone else flatly stated, "I know this fellow is one of Jesus' disciples, for both are from Galilee."

But Peter said, "Man, I don't know what you are talking about." And as he said the words, a rooster crowed.

At that moment Jesus turned and looked at Peter. Then Peter remembered what he had said—"Before the rooster crows tomorrow morning, you will deny me three times." And Peter walked out of the courtyard, crying bitterly. Luke 22:54-62

There aren't very many Christians at my school, and I'm kind of embarrassed about admitting I am one. Do I have to come out and let the whole world know I've become a Christian?

High school guys and girls wear letter jackets that tell the world they're athletes. The jacket also identifies them with a specific school, sport, and group of athletes. Most people wear it with pride. They have accomplished something, and they want other people to know.

Identifying yourself as a Christian, however, is not always real popular. Peter found that out when he was confronted by the people who were trying to get warm around the fire. Although he had been with Jesus for three years, and was one of his best friends, he denied even knowing who Jesus was!

Peter was afraid, he was embarrassed, and he wasn't really sure he wanted the world to know about his association with Jesus. But something happened during the next two months that convinced him he would never be ashamed of Jesus again (you can read about what he did in the first four chapters of the book of Acts).

When you're a new Christian, it's hard to identify yourself with Christ because you don't know him very well. It's like striking up a friendship with the new kid at school. Although you want to be his friend, sometimes you hold back because you aren't sure how popular he's going to be. Some people will even quit talking to a person just because he's not in the popular crowd.

Jesus understands our fears about identifying with him. There are situations where it is tough to admit we're his followers. He's also patient enough to wait until we're confident in our relationship with him before we begin to speak out for him. But I can imagine it kind of disappoints him a little, too.

Most new Christians go through a process to get to where they aren't embarrassed about admitting they're believers in Christ. For some people it takes years; for others it may happen the moment they believe in him. Something clicks that absolutely convinces them that Jesus Christ really is alive. It could be the feeling of being forgiven; it could be a miraculous answer to prayer; it could be that someone they know has changed so much that only God could have done the changing. For some, it might be a quiet realization that the Bible is accurate and everything Jesus said about himself is true.

God's expectation is not that you get on the P.A. system at school as soon as it happens and make the "big announcement." His expectation is that you'll be ready in case anyone asks you about your faith.

"Quietly trust yourself to Christ your Lord and if anybody asks why you believe as you do, be ready to tell him, and do it in a gentle and respectful way" (1 Peter 3:15).

(Solomon loved the Lord and followed all of his father David's instructions except that he continued to sacrifice in the hills and to offer incense there.) The most famous of the hilltop altars was at Gibeon, and now the king went there and sacrificed one thousand burnt offerings! The Lord appeared to him in a dream that night and told him to ask for anything he wanted, and it would be given to him!

Solomon replied, "You were wonderfully kind to my father David because he was honest and true and faithful to you, and obeyed your commands. And you have continued your kindness to him by giving him a son to succeed him. O Lord my God, now you have made me the king instead of my father David, but I am as a little child who doesn't know his way around. And here I am among your own chosen people, a nation so great that there are almost too many people to count! Give me an understanding mind so that I can govern your people well and know the difference between what is right and what is wrong. For who by himself is able to carry such a heavy responsibility?"

The Lord was pleased with his reply and was glad that Solomon had asked for wisdom. So he replied, "Because you have asked for wisdom in governing my people and haven't asked for a long life, or riches for yourself, or the defeat of your enemies—yes, I'll give you what you asked for! I will give you a wiser mind than anyone else has ever had or ever will have! And I will also give you what you didn't ask for—riches and honor! And no one in all the world will be as rich and famous as you for the rest of your life! And I will give you a long life if you follow me and obey my laws as your father David did." 1 Kings 3:3-14

With so many things out there that I want and so many things I know I need, how do I know what to pray for?

Do you realize your mom is faced with the same question every time she goes to the grocery store? She knows what you want to eat, but she buys what you need to eat. Her experience as a "home engineer" keeps you healthy!

God also wants you to be healthy. He knows exactly what to give you and when to give it to you. Jesus said:

> "If a child asks his father for a loaf of bread, will he be given a stone instead? If he asks for fish, will he be given a poisonous snake? Of course not! And if you hardhearted, sinful men know how to give good gifts to your children, won't your Father in heaven even more certainly give good gifts to those who ask him for them?" (Matthew 7:9-11)

Your mother was probably very glad when you asked for an apple for a snack instead of ice cream (has that day come?). It shows that you're becoming aware of what it will take to keep yourself healthy. Though ice cream tastes better, apples are far better for you.

Our requests to God can sometimes be very selfish, centered only on what we want and not on what we need. God the Father longs for the day when we ask him for what we really need or, better yet, what others need.

Solomon had the privilege of asking for anything he wanted from God. Of all of the choices available to him, Solomon made the one that was most pleasing to God. He asked for wisdom. God responded by giving Solomon more wisdom than any other man, and God gave him riches and honor as well so that others could benefit from the wisdom God gave him.

Selfish prayers are rarely answered yes by God because he loves us too much. Although a child whines for candy an hour before dinner, a wise parent will always say no.

The best things to pray for are those that will ultimately help other people. Good examples are character qualities (such as patience, self-control, gentleness) that will help you get along better with other people and will point others toward Christ. Another example is the health of someone who is sick (James 5:14-16).

When you have needs, however, you should never be afraid to ask God to meet them. He loves to answer the prayers of his children!

If young toughs tell you, "Come and join us"—turn your back on them! Proverbs 1:10

It always seems like I'm giving in to my friends. Lots of times I end up doing stuff I know a Christian shouldn't do. How do I stand up to the pressure?

If every young person had a dollar for every time friends said to "come along," most could pay for college!

Being included feels great. And everyone needs friends. But friends don't always have our welfare at heart. In fact, sometimes they only want us to join them so they can feel better about doing whatever it is they want to do.

But is it really pressure?

When someone invites you to go with him to a questionable (or bad) situation and you give in, you haven't just "succumbed" to peer pressure. You've *chosen* to do something wrong and have concealed your true identity.

We hide our real character, hoping to be liked by a group or person. We want to be accepted. Of course, this often works. If it didn't, people wouldn't do it!

We are all tempted to bend in order for someone to like us. During the teenage years, the pressure can be intense. It's the hungry urge to do what others are doing in order to fit in.

But God wants to provide the inner muscle you'll need to combat the outer pressure you feel. Ask him to give you the courage and strength to say no.

He also wants to teach you *what* to do. Remember when Mom or Dad taught you to do something like bake cookies or start a lawn mower? They didn't just tell you to do it. They showed you how.

God shows us how to act through the teaching and stories in the Bible.

Commands like, "Don't copy the behavior and customs of this world, but be a new and different person with a fresh newness in all you do and think" (Romans 12:2), need to be read to understand

God's heart. But examples from throughout the Bible will also help.

Joseph ran from his temptation (Genesis 39:12), and Daniel prayed his way through his (Daniel 6:10). And sometimes we just have to realize that the consequences are not worth the risk.

The whole Bible was given to us by inspiration from God and is useful to teach us what is true and to make us realize what is wrong in our lives; it straightens us out and helps us do what is right. It is God's way of making us well prepared at every point, fully equipped to do good to everyone. 2 Timothy 3:16-17

Who wrote the Bible, and how do I know if it really came from God?

God gave the words in the Bible by working in the minds of his chosen writers. Then these men wrote down what he wanted.

The Bible contains sixty-six books, written by about forty authors at various points in history. Many of the "books" are actually letters.

If you know a mathematician, ask him or her the probability of sixty-six separate documents, written over a period of fifteen hundred years, by forty different authors, not having any contradictions.

He'd have to conclude what you've described is mathematically impossible. Yet that's what God did as he wrote and arranged the Bible.

The theme, the history, the way the Bible reveals God's character, and, especially, the way it describes God's way of bringing salvation to mankind, are consistent throughout.

More important than how we got the Bible is why. God gave the Bible to us to prepare us for anything, in order that we might do good to everyone.

God's Word also serves as our offensive weapon against all of the problems we encounter. "For whatever God says to us is full of living power: it is sharper than the sharpest dagger, cutting swift and deep into our innermost thoughts and desires with all their parts, exposing us for what we really are" (Hebrews 4:12).

God is in the business of molding our character and strengthening us for future use. He's given us all of the resources for strength we'll ever need, in the Bible.

O Jehovah, God of my salvation, I have wept before you day and night. Now hear my prayers; oh, listen to my cry, for my life is full of troubles, and death draws near. They say my life is ebbing out—a hopeless case. They have left me here to die, like those slain on battlefields, from whom your mercies are removed.

You have thrust me down to the darkest depths. Your wrath lies heavy on me; wave after wave engulfs me. You have made my friends to loathe me, and they have gone away. I am in a trap with no way out. My eyes grow dim with weeping. Each day I beg your help; O Lord, I reach my pleading hands to you for mercy.

Soon it will be too late! Of what use are your miracles when I am in the grave? How can I praise you then? Can those in the grave declare your lovingkindness? Can they proclaim your faithfulness? Can the darkness speak of your miracles? Can anyone in the Land of Forgetfulness talk about your help?

O Lord, I plead for my life and will keep on pleading day by day. O Jehovah, why have you thrown my life away? Why are you turning your face from me and looking the other way? From my youth I have been sickly and ready to die. I stand helpless before your terrors. Your fierce wrath has overwhelmed me. Your terrors have cut me off. They flow around me all day long. Lover, friend, acquaintance—all are gone. There is only darkness everywhere.
Psalm 88

Does God get tired of hearing about our troubles? I get frustrated when I struggle with the same problems over and over.

Do you know someone who complains a lot? Perhaps you have a little brother or sister, a friend, or an acquaintance at school who is always complaining. Complainers aren't much fun to be around.

Complaining means we aren't happy with what's going on around us. Complaining also shines the spotlight on us for a while, and people give us attention. Sometimes, that's all we really wanted in the first place!

If you've ever read through the Psalms, you've seen that David seems to complain a lot! He's always in some sort of trouble, and he wants God to get him out of it. Sound familiar?

The motivation behind our complaining is the key issue. When surrounded by enemies, David cried to God for protection. He had nowhere else to turn. Although this may seem like complaining, it actually is a very honest way to pray. God never gets tired of hearing us and coming to our rescue if we need his help.

But sometimes when we complain or ask God for help it's because we have made wrong choices that have gotten us in trouble. Our natural response is to ask God to get us out of it. Although God always listens to us, he knows that the solution is not found in his coming to the rescue.

Instead we must ask for forgiveness and seek his help in changing the behavior that caused the problem in the first place. Some troubles are best solved by being humble and admitting we were wrong.

But if trouble comes from people or situations that are beyond our control, God is not only quick to hear, but also quick to answer. Either he will provide the internal resources necessary to handle the problem ("God's peace which is far more wonderful than the human mind can understand," Phil. 4:7) or he will provide the way of escape.

Many others have faced exactly the same problems before you. And no temptation is irresistible. You can trust God to keep the temptation from becoming so strong that you can't stand up against it, for he has promised this and will do what he says. He will show you how to escape temptation's power so that you can bear up patiently against it. (1 Corinthians 10:13)

*Long ago God spoke in many different ways to our fathers
through the prophets [in visions, dreams, and even face to face],
telling them little by little about his plans.*

*But now in these days he has spoken to us through his Son to
whom he has given everything, and through whom he made the
world and everything there is.*

*God's Son shines out with God's glory, and all that God's Son
is and does marks him as God. He regulates the universe by the
mighty power of his command. He is the one who died to cleanse
us and clear our record of all sin, and then sat down in highest
honor beside the great God of heaven.* Hebrews 1:1-3

**I've heard so many different opinions on what God is really
like that I'm beginning to wonder if someone can ever know.
Is there any way to know for sure?**

Have you ever assembled a complicated jigsaw puzzle? If so, you
know how important the picture on the box is. As you put the puzzle
together, you use the picture as a reference, your guide.

But what if you had the wrong box top, and the picture didn't
match the puzzle? The puzzle would be nearly impossible to assem-
ble (at least until you realized the mistake).

People throughout the world are trying to put the "God puzzle"
together. But often they're trying to match the pieces to the wrong
picture!

God isn't trying to hide. He has clearly shown the world what he
is like, through nature, through the Bible, and especially through
Christ.

Jesus said it plainly, "I and the Father are one" (John 10:30).

Even when he was asked point blank by Philip, he was straightfor-
ward in his reply. "Don't you even yet know who I am, Philip, even
after all this time I have been with you? Anyone who has seen me has
seen the Father! So why are you asking to see him?" John 14:9.

It doesn't get more obvious than that! To know what God is like,
all you have to do is look at Jesus.

People get their God-pictures from TV preachers; friends who say they believe in God but never act like it; religious relatives; coaches who pray before games and then swear the paint off of the walls at half-time; and so forth. These are pictures of God that aren't anything like what he's really like. No wonder they can't put the puzzle together.

That's why it's so important not to settle for hearsay when it comes to finding out what God is like. Instead, look at the right picture—look at Christ.

But Moses said, "They won't believe me! They won't do what I tell them to. They'll say, 'Jehovah never appeared to you!'" Exodus 4:1

I'm having trouble letting other people know I'm a Christian. I'm afraid they will laugh at me or ask a question I can't answer.

The Bible is filled with examples of people who faced the choice of either being courageous or letting their fears tell them how to act. Learning about the courage of people in the Bible is one good reason to read it every day. The examples we find in the Bible can give us the strength to step out in faith and do things that may *at first* seem very frightening.

In Exodus 3, God had just finished speaking with Moses through a burning bush. Although this was an incredible miracle, Exodus 4 relates how Moses was afraid people wouldn't believe that God had actually spoken to him. He had to choose between giving in to his fears or facing them head on. Eventually, Moses chose to draw courage from God and completed the task God had given him.

Whether it's riding a bike for the first time, going down a steep hill on a skateboard, or driving a car, there's always an element of the unknown that can only be overcome by doing what you think is frightening. Character and skill are developed by repeating an action until you can do it well enough to enjoy it. This is true with everything from snow skiing to volleyball—and it's true in telling your best friends on earth about your Friend in heaven.

God doesn't expect you to know all the answers. When the apostle Peter was confronted by the hostile religious leaders of the day who told him to stop talking about Jesus, he answered, "We cannot stop telling about the wonderful things we saw Jesus do and heard him say" (Acts 4:20). He had learned the joy of sharing his faith in Christ so much that he couldn't help but share what he knew.

You have the privilege and the responsibility of sharing what you've learned and what God has done in your life. If you don't know the answer, you can always say, "That's a good question. Can I find out the answer and get back with you tomorrow?"

The key to Moses' decision to obey God's command to be his spokesman for the Israelites was his remembering when God first spoke to him. The burning bush experience and God's continuing miracles gave Moses the courage to face incredible obstacles.

"If you love me, obey me. . . ."Jesus replied, "Because I will only reveal myself to those who love me and obey me. The Father will love them too, and we will come to them and live with them."
John 14:15, 23

If I obey God like I read I'm supposed to, will I get anything more than a clear conscience?

Although a clear conscience doesn't seem like much these days, some psychologists say that 50 percent of the people in mental hospitals could go home if they knew they were forgiven. There are real advantages in keeping a clear conscience before God.

Obedience to God will always have a reward, but it is also a command (John 14:15). This means it's our choice to either obey or disobey. The story of Abraham and Isaac is a great example of the rewards of obedience.

To most fathers, the command to sacrifice a son would clearly be one to disobey. Yet Abraham loved God so much that he trusted him, even with the future of his only son. Luke 22:39-46 tells of the choice Jesus faced when his Father asked him to give his life for the sins of the world.

The point is that Abraham needed to be tested by God to see if he was worthy of being the father of faith for the entire world. Abraham proved himself worthy by his obedience.

As a result, Isaac was spared, and Abraham's faith became the example for everyone seeking to know how to please God (see Hebrews 11:1-2; 17-19).

God rewards his children for their obedience. "You can never please God without faith, without depending on him. Anyone who wants to come to God must believe that there is a God and that he rewards those who sincerely look for him" (Hebrews 11:6).

Sometimes the rewards are immediate; other times God chooses to delay them. It's usually during those times when God chooses to delay our rewards that we begin to wonder if obedience to God is really worth it.

When God delays his rewards, he is testing us to see if we are obeying him out of love, or if we are obeying him for what we'll receive. God can't be manipulated into giving us things we aren't ready to handle. Sometimes we need to be tested first in smaller areas to show that we can handle larger rewards or responsibilities without becoming prideful.

Obey God, and leave the rewards to him.

For my people have done two evil things: They have forsaken me, the Fountain of Life-giving Water; and they have built for themselves broken cisterns that can't hold water! Jeremiah 2:13

My mom used to go to church a lot, but she doesn't anymore. What can I do to get her to give God more attention?

Going from a close relationship with Christ to total neglect is like going from a two-wheeled bike to one with training wheels. It seems safer, but it's not half the fun.

As a Christian, you'll see many people start out strong in their walk with God, but for some reason, they'll fade and eventually drop off.

But remember, the Christian life is not a sprint—it's a long-distance race, a marathon. How you start is not nearly as important as how you finish.

In a long race, many people get weary of waiting for the prize and decide to drop out. Your mother sounds like an example of that type. She seems to have turned her attention elsewhere, forgetting about the race altogether.

As this verse says, when people reject God, they need other things to hold life together. But those other things are just "broken water pots" that don't hold anything of value.

And like the person who goes back to the bike with training wheels because it's safer, some people allow distractions to push God aside.

If people believe that the Christian life means having their problems solved immediately, always being treated right by people, never having doubts about the future, having prayers always answered within a week, and always being entertained in church, then people are pursuing the wrong goal. They'll be disappointed, grow tired, and tend to drop out.

But if our goal is simply getting to know the God who created us and loved us enough to die on a cross to save us from sin, then we'll never get tired of the faith. There's always something new to discover about the richness and depth of God's love for us.

Finally, if our goal is to change a *selfish* character into a *selfless* character, the race will never seem too long.

Most people are impatient, with God, themselves, and others. If something doesn't happen immediately, they go on to something else. This happens in friendships, jobs, marriages—and it happens with God.

Don't try to change your mom. She'll likely not appreciate it, no matter how good your motives are. Instead, give God permission to change you! Focus on how well you are doing.

Become more diligent in doing your chores and homework. Begin to treat your brothers and sisters better than you have. Pray for her to see these changes. Then give God time to work. Remember, he wants her to have a right relationship with him even more than you do.

For Demas has left me. He loved the good things of this life and went to Thessalonica. Crescens has gone to Galatia, Titus to Dalmatia. 2 Timothy 4:10

A friend of mine stopped coming to church because he said that God had stopped answering his prayers. How do I answer him?

Like Demas, who deserted Paul, many Christians have a what-have-you-done-for-me-lately type of faith in God. They are willing to trust him in the good times. But when trouble hits, they figure that since God seems to have "checked out on them," they will "check out on God."

Of course we often do this with people. When Mom or Dad fails to meet up to our expectations, we're tempted to think that they no longer care.

Because we live in a society where often we can get what we want when we want it, we may begin to think that God's only purpose is to meet our needs. Then when something doesn't work out—when we think that God hasn't come through for us—we turn away from him.

God is in the business of molding our character. One way he does this is by allowing us to go through tough times. When Paul wrote this letter, the church was going through intense persecution. Demas got tired of it and left. He wanted his comforts more than he wanted God's will.

Encourage your friend to change the what-have-you-done-for-me-lately attitude. And help him realize that God wants to build his character. God's goal is not to make us feel good, but to develop us into the kind of people he wants.

The people of Beroea were more open-minded than those in Thessalonica, and gladly listened to the message. They searched the Scriptures day by day to check up on Paul and Silas' statements to see if they were really so. Acts 17:11

I'm not the kind of person that can take everything at face value. I have to have more proof. Is it wrong to want to know the answers to questions I have about the Bible?

The Christians in Beroea were complimented by Luke, the writer of Acts, because "they searched the Scriptures day by day to check up on Paul and Silas' statements to see if they were really so."

Because being a Christian means accepting Christ's forgiveness by faith, some think we must believe everything just because another Christian said it.

What if someone told you that the best way to make friends was to wear the right makeup, wear the right clothes, play the "popular" sports, and watch the right TV shows?

Learning how to make friends begins when you're young, as you learn how to get along with other kids your own age. Later, you learn to choose your friends by the things you have in common with them, not by what they look like or what they own. The art of having friends and being a friend is learned over a number of years.

Getting your questions answered by studying the Bible is an important part of being a Christian. Although not every question can be answered, most of them can.

Some people are natural skeptics. They challenge everything in the Bible. But often they aren't looking for answers.

If, however, you have the prayerful heart of a seeker, God will help you unlock the secrets of his Word. "Ask, and you will be given what you ask for. Seek, and you will find. Knock, and the door will be opened. For everyone who asks, receives. Anyone who seeks, finds. If only you will knock, the door will open" (Matthew 7:7-8).

Keep asking your questions and looking for answers.

All who believe this know in their hearts that it is true. If anyone doesn't believe this, he is actually calling God a liar because he doesn't believe what God has said about his Son. And what is it that God has said? That he has given us eternal life, and that this life is in his Son. So whoever has God's Son has life; whoever does not have his Son does not have life. 1 John 5:10-12

I became a Christian at a big youth rally last fall. Afterwards, I felt great for a few days. I knew that having a relationship with God was something I wanted. But soon my good feelings went away. Did I lose him? Why didn't the good feelings stay around?

Picture yourself meeting your favorite TV or music superstar face to face. It would be an experience that you'd likely never forget. Yet over time you'd forget the intensity of the emotion you once felt. Would it mean that you did not actually meet this person? No, but it does illustrate that our feelings often come and go based on current experience.

Asking Jesus Christ into your life is far better than meeting another human, famous or not. What you've begun is a lifelong relationship with God who created everything. He actually wants to live in you so that you'll live forever *and* so others can see that he really loves them too.

In John 14:23 Jesus says, "I will only reveal myself to those who love me and obey me. The Father will love them too, and we will come to them and live with them." The phrase *live with them* actually means "build a mansion" in them. God wants to come into your life and make something extraordinary out of it. God has begun a process of molding your character to become more like that of Jesus Christ. Within this lifelong process will be some good feelings, but more often we will not have, or want, continual, intense excitement.

Getting to know someone as loving and forgiving as Jesus Christ is similar to other relationships you enjoy. There is the initial experience of meeting a person, followed by months and years of growing to appreciate his or her friendship and influence. Anything worthwhile takes time.

Once you've genuinely chosen to follow Jesus Christ you can never lose him. He will always be there in your life to guide and love you in the midst of all that our world may throw your way. This should outweigh your tendency to base your relationship with God on your up and down feelings.

So revere Jehovah and serve him in sincerity and truth. Put away forever the idols your ancestors worshiped when they lived beyond the Euphrates River and in Egypt. Worship the Lord alone. But if you are unwilling to obey the Lord, then decide today whom you will obey. Will it be the gods of your ancestors beyond the Euphrates or the gods of the Amorites here in this land? But as for me and my family, we will serve the Lord. Joshua 24:14-15

If Christ controls my life, where does my freedom of choice fit in?

One way that God demonstrated his love for us was by giving us the freedom of choice.

Someone once said, "There is a door to your heart that can only be opened from the inside."

You made the choice to open the door of your heart to Jesus Christ when you received him as Savior and Lord. Although his Spirit was at work prompting you to respond to his love, the choice was yours.

Imagine your life as a house. Jesus Christ knocked on the front door and you decided to let him in (Revelation 3:20). Where do you invite him next? Some Christians live their whole lives with Christ still standing in the entryway. Obviously this isn't a very good way to treat an invited guest.

During your entire life as a Christian, you use your God-given freedom of choice to invite him into the rest of your house (your life) or to leave him at the front door.

Although your life is much more complicated than a house, let's take the illustration one step further.

In your house you probably have rooms that need repair. The living room, for example, could represent your relationships at home. How does the room look? When problems occur in this room the solution is to ask the master carpenter, Jesus, for some renovation. Through his Word, other people, and the prodding of the Holy Spirit, God gently tells us how to make things right.

This passage in Joshua tells of his challenge to the nation of Israel:

"Then you must destroy all the idols you now own, and you must obey the Lord God of Israel" (Joshua 24:23). The Israelites were faced with a choice of whom they were going to serve. On this day, they chose to serve the living God instead of idols made by human hands.

Every day you'll be faced with the choice of serving God or something else. God loves you too much to take that choice away from you, even if it means you make the wrong choice.

He has given to you the privilege of having him come into every area of your life—your language, what you put in front of your eyes, what you listen to. Trust him to know what he's doing.

For God says, "I will destroy all human plans of salvation no matter how wise they seem to be, and ignore the best ideas of men, even the most brilliant of them." 1 Corinthians 1:19

I hear a lot about the "New Age." Some of my friends say they are in it. How is this different from what I believe as a Christian?

The most convenient religion is one you create yourself. And that is what the New Age movement does for people. It allows them to create whatever rules they want to have about God, their behavior, and how to make it to the next life.

And so *New Age* is impossible to define. But, generally, here is what most New-Agers believe:

They believe that God is everywhere and in everybody. Because we are humans, we all have a unity of spirit that allows us to be brothers no matter what. God is not good or bad. In fact, each person is a god. He or she is the center of the universe. Morality, therefore, isn't important (since God is not seen as either good or bad). But the mind and intellect are very important because, supposedly, a person has to think deep thoughts to understand these concepts.

They believe that "salvation" comes through reincarnation. This means coming back to life again in the form of someone else, again and again, until you get it right. (Reincarnation is a lie; the Bible is very clear on this point. See Hebrews 9:27.)

There are so many strains within the New Age movement that it's impossible to outline them all. But the key for this type of thinking are the beliefs that there is no personal God, that human beings are not sinful, and that the next life is assured in some form, no matter what you've done here on earth. This is a very convenient religion if you just want to do your own thing.

But listen to God: "The Lord says: Cursed is the man who puts his trust in mortal man and turns his heart away from God" (Jeremiah 17:5). When people set their own beliefs and thoughts up as more important than what God thinks, they are actually being cursed by him.

Temptation to think yourself out of a relationship with God is everywhere. Nearly every belief within the New Age movement allows you to become your own god. Eve was told by Satan that she would become like God if she ate of the fruit of the tree (Genesis 3:1-6). People are being told they can be god of their life if they will just look away from the one, true God.

The Bible must be our authority on what we are to believe about God, ourselves, and what it takes to be saved from our sin. If it isn't, everyone can create a religion to suit his or her own desires.

Call out the demon hordes you've worshiped all these years. Call on them to help you strike deep terror into many hearts again. You have advisers by the ton—your astrologers and stargazers, who try to tell you what the future holds. But they are as useless as dried grass burning in the fire. They cannot even deliver themselves! You'll get no help from them at all. Theirs is no fire to sit beside to make you warm! And all your friends of childhood days shall slip away and disappear, unable to help.
Isaiah 47:12-15

I used to look up my horoscope every day in the paper before a friend told me it was satanic. Do Christians believe in astrology?

There are many "windows" that may lead people into satanic influence. Horoscopes seem harmless, but they are not.

When Saul was King of Israel and in trouble, he consulted a medium (a witch) to gain knowledge of the future (see 1 Samuel 28). Many other passages deal with astrology, divination, wizards, sorcery, and soothsayers (see Deuteronomy 18:10-12; 2 Chronicles 33:6; Daniel 2:2; Acts 8:9; 16:16).

If Satan can get people to swallow a taste of darkness, one morsel at a time, eventually they may not recognize that they have just been fed a meal that will cause them to lose interest in God.

If Satan can convince people their horoscope can sometimes come true, their thirst to know God will be quenched—artificially quenched, but quenched nonetheless!

It's like the boy who tried to boil a frog. He filled up a beaker with water, put it on the Bunsen burner until it was boiling, and then put the frog in. Immediately the frog jumped out of the water. The way to boil a frog is to put it in cold water and then slowly turn up the heat. The frog will get used to its surroundings and put up with the increasing heat until it boils to death.

Satan would never get anyone to follow him if he revealed all his evil. Instead, he slowly opens windows of darkness until we're inside.

Rarely does someone become a cocaine addict or an alcoholic during the first time of experimentation. It takes time. Child molesters and sexual deviants are not born that way. They have exposed themselves to destructive pictures and thoughts that lead them to destroy their lives through sexual addictions.

Music and other media encourage us to adopt the values of Hollywood or of corrupt music groups. It is not always shockingly noticeable, but it is extremely effective in changing people's attitudes and eventually their actions—away from a relationship with the God who loves them.

This is the strategy: to capture our minds through one small compromise after another.

The best defense is to know the truth of the Word of God, so we can discern when we are being tempted by evil. God knows it is real. And Jesus came to destroy the works of the devil. Remember, "There is someone in your hearts who is stronger than any evil teacher in this wicked world" (1 John 4:4).

As they sat down to eat, he asked God's blessing on the food and then took a small loaf of bread and broke it and was passing it over to them, when suddenly—it was as though their eyes were opened—they recognized him! And at that moment he disappeared!

They began telling each other how their hearts had felt strangely warm as he talked with them and explained the Scriptures during the walk down the road. Within the hour they were on their way back to Jerusalem, where the eleven disciples and the other followers of Jesus greeted them with these words, "The Lord has really risen! He appeared to Peter!"

Then the two from Emmaus told their story of how Jesus had appeared to them as they were walking along the road and how they had recognized him as he was breaking the bread.
Luke 24:30-35

My church regularly does something called "Communion." What is it supposed to do for me?

What have you saved from a special event, because you wanted to remember how great that moment was? A ticket stub? A card? A trophy?

Ask your parents to take you through their "nostalgia boxes" sometime. They'll say things like: "This is the varsity letter I won my senior year for swimming," or, "Here is the ring box that contained the ring your father gave me the day he proposed."

Certain items help us remember special moments in our lives.

When Jesus was about to die, be raised, and return to heaven, he wanted to leave his followers something tangible to remember him by. He could have left a physical item like a robe or a cup. But people would begin to worship the object instead of God, and the object would be seen by just a few. So instead, he left an "act," something to do.

Communion (the Lord's Supper, Eucharist) is that act—a word picture of what Jesus did on the cross. There, his body was broken and his blood was shed . . . for us.

This passage says that Jesus was recognized "as he was breaking the bread" (v. 35). Communion helps us recognize who Jesus is and that he is with us as we worship.

And because Communion is celebrated by believers throughout the world, it is a unifying act.

And because we retell the message of Christ's death, we are reminded that he is going to return someday to take us to heaven. (See also 1 Corinthians 11:23-26).

Christians will always need those reminders. There are too many distractions that cause us to lose our focus on what really matters in this life. Communion briefly reminds us that real *life* revolves not around us, but around one incredible act of love at a certain time in history. "This is my body . . . This is my blood . . . do this in remembrance of me."

But when you had eaten and were satisfied, then you became proud and forgot me. Hosea 13:6

People around me at school don't act like they need God. How can I share my faith in Christ with them if they don't feel a need to even talk about him, let alone get to know him?

Rarely will people want a relationship with someone if they feel like they don't need him or her. The Bible is filled with stories of people who have actively rejected God because they felt no need—their lives were going so well. You may know someone like that.

But when things are rough, people quickly pin the blame on God. This makes as much sense as a six-year-old hitting himself on the thumb with a hammer and then blaming his dad.

"I saw you use your hammer once, Dad. And even though you told me not to use it, I chose to anyway. It's your job to make sure I never hurt myself with it. If I do hurt myself, it'll be your fault!"

People do the same with God.

"I'm going to take my life and run it the way I want to, God; but if things go wrong, it's your fault!"

Though you can't create within someone a need for God, here are some things you can do:

- Pray for your friends to be faced with a situation where they will have to look to God for help. The Prodigal Son had to feed pigs and eat their food before he finally came to his senses and returned to his father (see Luke 15:11-32). If someone really wants to go his own way, there's usually nothing you can do besides pray for him.
- Be ready to help your friends when they do have needs. Keep the friendship bridges strong enough so that your friends will come to you for help. Then you can point them to Christ. Seek the help of a mature Christian friend for advice on how to do this best.
- Look for people who are already hurt and share the Good News with them.

- Watch out for your own heart. The Bible is clear that certain things can cause us to take our eyes off of God.

"Trust in your money and down you go! Trust in God and flourish as a tree!" (Proverbs 11:28).

"Before every man there lies a wide and pleasant road that seems right but ends in death" (Proverbs 14:12).

The "easy" life of living separated from God is exactly how Satan wants us to live. The stakes are high. Being separated from God in this life affects our eternity in the next.

And so the Lord says, "Since these people say they are mine but they do not obey me, and since their worship amounts to mere words learned by rote, therefore I will take awesome vengeance on these hypocrites and make their wisest counselors as fools."
Isaiah 29:13-14

It seems every other month my dad is complaining about seeing another TV preacher getting into trouble or a local pastor who molested someone. What do I say to people who point to the hypocrites in this world as their reason for giving God the cold shoulder?

Unfortunately, even some of God's own children can act shamefully. In fact, there's probably not a Christian alive who, at one time or another, hasn't betrayed God by his or her actions.

The word *hypocrisy* means "playacting," acting like someone else while claiming to be a certain type of person.

God is pretty upset at hypocrites, those who claim to be followers, but really aren't.

Jesus said, "More than anything else, beware of these Pharisees and the way they pretend to be good when they aren't. But such hypocrisy cannot be hidden forever. It will become as evident as yeast in dough. Whatever they have said in the dark shall be heard in the light, and what you have whispered in the inner rooms shall be broadcast from the housetops for all to hear!" (Luke 12:1-3).

When the final act draws to a close, some of the first to receive God's wrath will be those who have been playacting with God. He's not impressed; they will be judged.

There is literally nothing you can do to prevent strangers from misrepresenting Christ. The only person you can keep from being a hypocrite is you.

Here are some ways to keep from becoming a hypocrite:

First, watch closely your own actions (see 2 Corinthians 13:5). Though God reads your heart, other people see your actions first. If what you do doesn't match what you tell others you believe, get ready to be called a hypocrite.

Second, don't come down on other people too hard. Remember, the only difference between you and those who aren't Christians is that you have received the gift of forgiveness.

Third, be quick to admit it when you make a mistake. True humility is rare in our culture, but for some reason people are drawn to those who can readily admit their mistakes. It's called being genuine.

After I have poured out my rains again, I will pour out my Spirit upon all of you! Your sons and daughters will prophesy; your old men will dream dreams, and your young men see visions. And I will pour out my Spirit even on your slaves, men and women alike, and put strange symbols in the earth and sky—blood and fire and pillars of smoke.

The sun will be turned into darkness and the moon to blood before the great and terrible Day of the Lord shall come.

Everyone who calls upon the name of the Lord will be saved; even in Jerusalem some will escape, just as the Lord has promised, for he has chosen some to survive. Joel 2:28-32

I wish God would do more "miracle" type things in my life. I've heard people talk about what he's done for them—incredible stuff! Why don't amazing things happen more often?

Miracles and "amazing things" are great to have, but the best miracle God could ever perform is the miracle of salvation.

That God has actually chosen to forgive our sin and live inside us is an incredible miracle. We should thank him for that every day. But often we forget.

Some teachers of the law once came to Jesus and asked him "to show them a miracle" (Matthew 12:38). He answered that they wouldn't see any greater miracle than his being dead and buried, staying three days in the ground, and then coming back to life! But they weren't satisfied.

The real question is, what kind of miracles do you want God to do in your life?

Do you want him to give you *A*s in subjects you haven't studied for? Allow you to score the winning touchdown so people will notice you? Perform some healing of an injury or sickness to "prove" he's still in your life? If so, you'll be disappointed. He doesn't do anything just to prove he exists—beyond, of course, what he's already done.

But if you want to see him do miracles in the lives of those around you, stand back. That's the kind he specializes in.

You'll find that the most exciting miracles are when God uses you to lead someone else to him. Those kinds are better because they lead to something eternal.

The longer you follow Christ, the more you'll see things happen. But when the eternal destiny of someone is changed, and God chose to use you to have a part in it, you'll experience a "high" unlike any other. The goal is to be used by God. The feelings are just a bonus.

Ask God to use you to perform the greatest miracle of all—to lead someone to Christ.

One of the teachers of religion who was standing there listening to the discussion realized that Jesus had answered well. So he asked, "Of all the commandments, which is the most important?"

Jesus replied, "The one that says, 'Hear, O Israel! The Lord our God is the one and only God. And you must love him with all your heart and soul and mind and strength.'

"The second is: 'You must love others as much as yourself.' No other commandments are greater than these."

The teacher of religion replied, "Sir, you have spoken a true word in saying that there is only one God and no other. And I know it is far more important to love him with all my heart and understanding and strength, and to love others as myself, than to offer all kinds of sacrifices on the altar of the Temple."

Realizing this man's understanding, Jesus said to him, "You are not far from the Kingdom of God." And after that, no one dared ask him any more questions. Mark 12:28-34

Why are there so many rules to go by after you become a Christian?

If you want to survive being lost in the wilderness for more than a night, there are certain things you must *have* and *do* in order to make it out safely.

The basics you need are a knife, warm clothes, and some matches. These will help you find food, stay warm, make a shelter, and start a fire. Basic survival is the first order of business when you're lost.

The one instrument that's key for providing direction out of the wilderness is a compass. Without it, most could only guess which direction they should go. Pursuing a wrong course could delay finding safety to the point where your life might be in danger.

Survival as a Christian, especially in today's wilderness, also depends on things that will not only provide basic survival but will give the direction needed for future "safety."

The elements of survival, "the rules" you talked about, can vary, depending on what type of Christian group you're a part of. Most groups use Scripture to back up what they believe are basic survival ingredients.

Examples of issues that are most disagreed upon within the Christian world are how much exposure to the secular media we should have (music, movies, TV); whether the opposite sexes should have physical contact while dating (hugging, kissing); when people reach twenty-one, whether they should drink any form of alcohol, even if they aren't wanting to get drunk.

The groups who say no to all of the above have likely learned, through tough experiences, that involvement in these areas can lead to actions that would be extremely harmful to a growing Christian. Scripturally, there is a strong case to be made for this type of conclusion.

What needs to be considered, above human opinions, is *what God really expects of me.*

When Jesus was confronted with a similar question, his response was simple. He said to "love God with all your heart and soul and mind and strength," and to "love others as much as yourself. No other commandments are greater than these."

To love God means to obey him (John 14:15). *Obedience* is a word that we don't normally like to talk about. We like to do our own thing. Yet it's the key to showing God we are really serious about following him. Loving God means not just allowing him into our lives but finding out what his heart is on the issues that can trip us up.

Loving others as much as ourselves also takes a lot of work. Most psychologists agree that 90 percent of the people spend 90 percent of their time thinking how they can get their own needs met. We are a very selfish people.

These two commandments by Jesus serve as a compass to our lives. Without them, we would wander in the wrong direction and would never really understand what it means to be a Christian.

The rest of the "rules" that we can get tired of hearing about are survival skills. They are not an end in themselves. They only push us closer to the goal of loving God (by obeying him) and loving others as we love ourselves.

66

Now there were four lepers sitting outside the city gates.

"Why sit here until we die?" they asked each other. "We will starve if we stay here and we will starve if we go back into the city; so we might as well go out and surrender to the Syrian army. If they let us live, so much the better; but if they kill us, we would have died anyway."

So that evening they went out to the camp of the Syrians, but there was no one there! (For the Lord had made the whole Syrian army hear the clatter of speeding chariots and a loud galloping of horses and the sounds of a great army approaching. "The king of Israel has hired the Hittites and Egyptians to attack us," they cried out. So they panicked and fled into the night, abandoning their tents, horses, donkeys, and everything else.)

When the lepers arrived at the edge of the camp they went into one tent after another, eating, drinking wine, and carrying out silver and gold and clothing and hiding it. "Finally they said to each other, "This isn't right. This is wonderful news, and we aren't sharing it with anyone! Even if we wait until morning, some terrible calamity will certainly fall upon us; come on, let's go back and tell the people at the palace." 2 Kings 7:3-9

Which is more important to do, *live* like a Christian or *tell* others about my new faith in Christ?

Try to remember the best Christmas present you ever received. What did you do after your family was through opening presents? More than likely, you called your best friend to tell him about your present.

Forgiveness from sin is the greatest gift you will ever receive! It's impossible to keep quiet about it if you truly recognize how important this free gift really is.

Compare the four men with leprosy who discovered the empty camp to a group of five-year-olds waking up Christmas morning with more presents than they could ever open! The joy and amazement the lepers experienced was beyond their wildest dreams. God had given them something that was simply too wonderful to keep to themselves.

Unfortunately some people take for granted the gift of salvation through Jesus Christ. These are often the people who say little about their faith.

For other Christians, having Christ as Savior is the most exciting present they have ever been given! Of course, having a present does not automatically mean that others will know about it. We must tell them.

The choice the men with leprosy faced was probably tough to make because the disease separated them from other people.

Our sin is like leprosy. We can't always tell its effects, but left unchecked, the disease gets progressively worse. Having our sin cleansed when we receive the gift of forgiveness through Christ should bring the same joy a leper would have when suddenly cleansed.

Our response in thankfulness to God, we hope, should not cause us to just hold the gift but to give it to all who will take it.

Well son, you can either breathe or have a heartbeat, whichever is more important to you.

Now you have every grace and blessing; every spiritual gift and power for doing his will are yours during this time of waiting for the return of our Lord Jesus Christ. And he guarantees right up to the end that you will be counted free from all sin and guilt on that day when he returns. God will surely do this for you, for he always does just what he says, and he is the one who invited you into this wonderful friendship with his Son, even Christ our Lord.
1 Corinthians 1:7-9

My *Christian* **friends are dragging me down. How am I supposed to grow as a Christian if these friends aren't really trying to do anything with their faith?**

Because God is the one who "invited you into this wonderful friendship with his Son," he shares the responsibility for making sure you grow in your faith. He has no intention of abandoning you in this area.

Many people have been touched by divorce in one way or another. Kids of divorced parents are often determined to make sure that their own marriage is a success. They seek out positive role models to observe, and they pore over numerous resources about having a quality marriage.

But the opposite also can be true. Kids who grow up without a good model of what a family is supposed to look like can easily repeat their parents' mistakes.

Because your friends are acting like they have "divorced God," you are faced with a choice. Will you learn from their mistakes and search out people and other resources to help you succeed in your relationship with Christ? Or will you follow their lead and turn your back on God as well? If you're serious about giving God every chance to make himself real in your life, consider these suggestions:

First, pray for your friends and for an opportunity to talk to them about the situation. Don't worry about how much you've blown it by participating in whatever they've done. It's more important to think about your future than to dwell on the past. Next, go to one of your

Christian friends, perhaps the leader of the group, and say something like: "I really want to give God a shot, but you're not helping much. I need your help. Can I count on you?" If he says yes, it worked! If he doesn't, go to another friend and tell him the same thing. If no one responds, wait a week or two and start the process again, trusting that God has been working in their hearts. Or find some new friends you can count on. Maybe that's the answer God has for you.

Remember, God is faithful. He knows that you need friends and a group to hang around with. The last thing you need is people who are heading in the wrong direction.

So he got back into the boat. The man who had been possessed by the demons begged Jesus to let him go along. But Jesus said no.

"Go home to your friends," he told him, "and tell them what wonderful things God has done for you; and how merciful he has been."

So the man started off to visit the Ten Towns of that region and began to tell everyone about the great things Jesus had done for him; and they were awestruck by his story. Mark 5:18-20

Now that I am a Christian, how should I act around my friends and family who are not?

The most important thing you have going for you in both sets of relationships is that you already have a "relational bridge" in place. They knew what your life was like before you met Christ. Now they will have the chance to see you afterwards.

Jesus recognized that this was the case with the man he had just cleansed from demon possession. So he sent him back to his home instead of asking him to leave those who knew him best.

Another passage calls us Christ's ambassadors to our world (2 Corinthians 5:17-20). This means we are his handpicked representatives. If people want to know what God is like, all they have to do is look at us.

God doesn't expect you to be perfect, but he does expect your faith to grow (Romans 10:17) and that you try to live more like Jesus Christ would each day (Romans 12:1-2).

It's progress—not perfection—that people around you will be able to relate to. Progress may be slow at first, but eventually, if you're giving areas of your life to Christ's control, people will begin to notice the change. Hopefully, they'll also start to ask questions about your new faith.

Although you may "feel" inadequate answering some of their questions, your responsibility is only to share what God has done for you and what you have learned, not to be the Bible answer man.

It's just as important (and biblical!) to share and live your faith as a new Christian as it is to be more mature in the faith or a Bible scholar. God is not limited by our lack of knowledge.

Like the Gadarene demoniac, whose life Jesus changed, you may have faced many unique hardships. But, as a new Christian, your changed life will have a greater impact on your friends, those with whom relational bridges have already been built, than will the words of a stranger, however eloquently he may speak.

So also the Lord can rescue you and me from the temptations that surround us, and continue to punish the ungodly until the day of final judgment comes. 2 Peter 2:9

Is temptation a sin? If it is, I'm sinning all the time. It seems like thoughts are always coming into my mind to do things that are wrong.

If temptation were a sin, then Jesus was a sinner (see Matthew 4:1-11 for the story of when Satan tempted Jesus in the wilderness). Temptation isn't a sin. It's the natural consequence of living in this world.

What leads to sin is following the path temptation wants us to take. If taken far enough, the path will cause us to think and do what's wrong.

Though temptation will always be present, we don't have to wave the white flag and admit defeat. We have the power to resist because the Holy Spirit lives in us.

God's Word also reminds us how to overcome temptation. First Corinthians 10:13 says "But remember this—the wrong desires that come into your life aren't anything new and different. Many others have faced exactly the same problems before you. And no temptation is irresistible. You can trust God to keep the temptation from becoming so strong that you can't stand up against it, for he has promised this and will do what he says. He will show you how to escape temptation's power so that you can bear up patiently against it."

Try to figure out where the way of escape occurs in this story:

You're at school and a friend asks you if you want to spend the night with some other guys and watch videos. You check with your folks, and, after you assure them there'll be no R-rated videos, they give the okay to let you go. Everything is cool, so far.

Once you arrive, you look at the stack of videos and notice that half of them are R-rated. You get your friend alone and ask him what the deal is. He says the other guys picked out the videos. Besides, everyone (but you) has seen them before, so he didn't think you'd mind.

Do you stay and go against what your parents want, just to go along with the group?

Let's say you stay. The next day Dad asks what movies you watched. Now you have to lie to stay out of trouble. So you lie. Unfortunately, however, Mom spoke with one of your friends' moms on the phone and found out there were R-rated movies at the sleep-over. Now you're grounded until age twenty-seven!

Where was the escape hatch to the temptation to disobey your parents? As soon as you found out that R-rated movies would be shown, you had two choices. You could have apologized to your friends, called your dad, and had him come pick you up. Or you could have gone to a different part of the house and done something else.

God always provides a way of escape in every circumstance. We choose whether to take his way out or to do things we know are wrong. If we stay close to God, we'll be more likely to resist and do what's right. We don't have to give in.

And now, brothers, as I close this letter, let me say this one more thing: Fix your thoughts on what is true and good and right. Think about things that are pure and lovely, and dwell on the fine, good things in others. Think about all you can praise God for and be glad about. Philippians 4:8

Before I became a Christian, I put my mind through some real garbage. How do I clean up my thought life?

Almost every school in America is equipped with computers. Most businesses remain competitive because they're able to access and store large amounts of information. Computers are serving nearly every segment of society. But they have one flaw—they are dependent on the programs and information put into them.

Your mind works like a computer. If it's programmed to think about crud, that's what will happen. If it's programmed to think about things that are healthy, you'll think healthy thoughts. It's as simple as that.

The hard part comes in trying to keep out the unhealthy thoughts. It doesn't take much to pollute a mind.

So what's God's solution? Reprogram the mind! For this job, there are no shortcuts. The more exposure to things that have polluted us, whether from bad movies, magazines, TV, music, concerts, or just the everyday conversation of friends who don't care what they say, the longer it will take to clear our minds and reprogram them.

The reprogramming process begins when we realize that destructive thoughts and images are trying to get a foothold in our mind, and we start kicking them out. The next step is choosing to dwell on what is positive and good.

The battle now is being waged in the thought life. Ask God to rescue you from destructive thoughts, and he will do it!

His apostles asked him what the story meant.

He replied, "God has granted you to know the meaning of these parables, for they tell a great deal about the Kingdom of God. But these crowds hear the words and do not understand, just as the ancient prophets predicted.

"This is its meaning: The seed is God's message to men. The hard path where some seed fell represents the hard hearts of those who hear the words of God, but then the devil comes and steals the words away and prevents people from believing and being saved. The stony ground represents those who enjoy listening to sermons, but somehow the message never really gets through to them and doesn't take root and grow. They know the message is true, and sort of believe for awhile; but when the hot winds of persecution blow, they lose interest. The seed among the thorns represents those who listen and believe God's words but whose faith afterwards is choked out by worry and riches and the responsibilities and pleasures of life. And so they are never able to help anyone else to believe the Good News.

"But the good soil represents honest, good-hearted people. They listen to God's words and cling to them and steadily spread them to others who also soon believe." Luke 8:9-15

There are so many things in my life that could pull me away from God. How can I make sure I'll always be "good soil"?

Insurance salespeople sell policies to protect people from financial losses from accident, catastrophe, or illness. When disaster strikes, the insured person will be reimbursed.

As a Christian, you need an insurance policy to protect you from spiritual disasters. Of course you can't buy this insurance, but God will give you a plan that will help "insure" you against your new faith being destroyed.

Skyscrapers must be carefully planned in order for them not to topple when a stiff wind hits. First, a huge hole is dug deep in the ground. Thousands of tons of concrete are poured, steel girders are welded into place, and everything is made to fit according to exact specifications. If the foundation is strong and straight, a strong building can be built on it.

The rest of the structure, however, must also be built strong, with the right materials fitted together in the right way at the right time.

The first phase in your life began when you accepted Christ's forgiveness and became a Christian. "And no one can ever lay any other real foundation than that one we already have—Jesus Christ" (1 Corinthians 3:11).

The second phase starts with the Word of God. If you study the Bible and have other Christians help you understand and apply it, your life in Christ will be strong. "There are various kinds of materials that can be used to build on that foundation. Some use gold and silver and jewels; and some build with sticks, and hay, or even straw!" (1 Corinthians 3:12).

If you are exposed to teaching that downplays God's Word, it's like building your life with sticks, hay, and straw. It will collapse when problems or persecution from friends and family arise (see Matthew 7:21-28).

To continue to build a solid Christian life, you should make sure that all you're hearing is lining up with what the Bible really says. You can do this by praying for direction, asking questions, and finding people who believe as you do that the Bible is God's blueprint for building a strong life.

But though Daniel knew about it, he went home and knelt down as usual in his upstairs bedroom, with its windows open toward Jerusalem, and prayed three times a day, just he always had, giving thanks to his God.

Then the men thronged to Daniel's house and found him praying there, asking favors of his God. They rushed back to the king and reminded him about his law. "Haven't you signed a decree," they demanded, "that permits no petitions to any God or man—except you—for thirty days? And anyone disobeying will be thrown to the lions?"

"Yes," the king replied, "it is a 'law of the Medes and Persians,' that cannot be altered or revoked."

Then they told the king, "That fellow Daniel, one of the Jewish captives, is paying no attention to you or your law. He is asking favors of his God three times a day."

Hearing this, the king was very angry with himself for signing the law and determined to save Daniel. He spent the rest of the day trying to think of some way to get Daniel out of this predicament.

In the evening the men came again to the king and said, "Your Majesty, there is nothing you can do. You signed the law, and it cannot be changed." Daniel 6:10-15

I'm involved in so many activities at school and church that lately I haven't had any time to spend with God. How do I keep from getting too busy for him?

God knows that you live in a busy world. But being busy is no excuse for ignoring him. And the pressures and demands on you will increase as you grow older. That's why you must decide *now* to do what's important and make your relationship with God your number one priority.

Busyness is a hard habit to break. People have a tendency to think they aren't doing what God wants if they're not rushing from one thing to the next. Even busyness with "Christian" things can be unhealthy, pulling us away from God and spiritual nourishment.

Daniel risked death to spend time with God. It's tough for many Christians to risk missing TV shows, friends, phone calls, and magazines to spend time with him. Somewhere, our priorities are mixed up. Unless they're brought back in line with what's really best for us—spending time alone with Christ—we'll always be running around, distracted from what is really important.

It's essential to learn this lesson early in your Christian life. The joy you can have, just spending time with Christ, is far greater than the feeling of being busy. Listen to this plea from Jesus.

"But you shouldn't be so concerned about perishable things like food. No, spend your energy seeking the eternal life that I, the Messiah, can give you. For God the Father has sent me for this very purpose" (John 6:27).

Dear brothers, is your life full of difficulties and temptations?
Then be happy, for when the way is rough, your patience has a
chance to grow. So let it grow, and don't try to squirm out of your
problems. For when your patience is finally in full bloom, then
you will be ready for anything, strong in character, full and
complete. James 1:2-4

My grandma has been a Christian for forty years. She has
faced so much trouble during those years I can't believe it.
Two husbands have died, one child, and her house recently
burned down. Why would God allow so much trouble to
come into one person's life?

No doubt you've seen weight lifters on TV or have friends who work
out with weights.

The goal of lifting weights, of course, is to develop the muscles
and make them stronger. But this muscle-building process involves
the muscles' being continually broken down.

At first, the strain of lifting causes the person to feel weak. In the
long run, however, it makes him or her strong.

Like a muscle, faith grows stronger when it's exercised than
during times of relative ease. That's why this passage says to be happy
when facing difficult trials and temptations.

One of God's goals for us is to learn to trust him more. When
Christians ask God for more faith, they are really asking for more
trials. God knows that only through this kind of "exercise" can their
faith be strengthened.

Eventually, James says, we will be "ready for anything, strong in
character, full and complete."

Another reason for trials and problems is found in 2 Corinthians 1:3-5—helping others. "What a wonderful God we have—he is
the Father of our Lord Jesus Christ, the source of every mercy, and
the one who so wonderfully comforts and strengthens us in our
hardships and trials. And why does he do this? So that when others
are troubled, needing our sympathy and encouragement, we can

pass on to them this same help and comfort God has given us. You can be sure that the more we undergo sufferings for Christ, the more he will shower us with his comfort and encouragement."

Helping someone else is probably the last thing we're thinking about when we're going through problems. But our success at coming through trials is very important to God. Then he can use us to pass along comfort and encouragement to others.

Some Christians are glad that they have few problems. Unfortunately, they won't have the opportunity to see their character grow stronger. And they won't receive the joy that comes when they help others.

Here is a summary of the events in the creation of the heavens and earth which the Lord God made.

There were no plants or grain sprouting up across the earth at first, for the Lord God hadn't sent any rain; nor was there anyone to farm the soil. (However, water welled up from the ground at certain places and flowed across the land.)

The time came when the Lord God formed a man's body from the dust of the ground and breathed into it the breath of life. And man became a living person. Genesis 2:4-7

When I read about creation and miracles in the Bible, I get confused. How do science and the Bible relate?

The Bible and science debate has raged for centuries. Conflicts arise when we try to look for spiritual answers from science or scientific answers from the Bible.

A former Vietnam POW told of the time he was allowed to send a cassette tape home to his family. Realizing that it might be the last communication he would ever have with those he loved, he made extensive notes on what he would cover before he began to make the tape. His goal was to communicate the most important things his family should know. To his wife, he talked of insurance, mortgages, child rearing, and relatives. To the kids, he personalized each message so that he touched on unique situations they would face the next few years as they grew up without him. To all of them he made sure he told how much he loved them.

This is exactly the purpose behind the Bible. God put sixty-six books together to let his creation know the most important things about life, about what to do in certain situations, and especially about the extent of his love for them.

For some reason he chose to leave out dinosaurs, fusion, and gravity (among other significant discoveries). Instead, he included stories of real people with real struggles who faced hardship and trials, many of whom conquered fears and circumstances because they realized that if God was for them, who could be against them!

Many other stories are included of those who rejected God and then experienced the tragic consequences.

Most of these biblical examples tell us much more about living, surviving, and prospering in a complicated society than science could ever hope to promise.

Your mind matters to God—he wants you to think. Never be afraid to ask tough questions about the Bible or the Christian faith. But also consider the appropriateness of each question: Is this the kind of question the Bible *should* answer? And do the same with science, asking the right questions.

Creation and the resurrection of Jesus Christ are two of the most important tenets of the Christian faith. Although they can't be duplicated in a laboratory, they also can't be proven to be false by science.

If God can create life from nothing, as well as raise a man from the dead, he can guide us through this life *and* the next. We can trust him.

I am giving all of it to you! Go in and possess it, for it is the land the Lord promised to your ancestors Abraham, Isaac, and Jacob, and all of their descendants. Deuteronomy 1:8

The Old Testament is long and sometimes boring. Why did God put it in the Bible?

Have you ever asked one of your grandparents to tell you his whole life story? You'd probably receive an all-day talk, full of wonderful stories. Though it would be fun for your grandparent, you'd likely be bored because you would hear too many facts that wouldn't relate to your life.

If, however, you just asked him to relate the top ten experiences that shaped his personality and helped him make it through life, it would only take an hour, it would be fascinating, and you'd learn a lot.

The Old Testament is not a detailed day-by-day account of history. Instead it is the story of the Jewish people. Their history points to Jesus Christ. Through this story, we see God's plan of sending his Son, Jesus, to die on the cross to pay the penalty for our sin.

Living in the twentieth century limits our appreciation of the fact that for three thousand years, the Old Testament has guided people from every walk of life. It was not just written for young people in the 1990s, but also for people who needed to hear from God in A.D. 320 Rome or A.D. 1540 Germany.

What this means is that not every story will affect you the way it has others through the years. But as you read through the Old Testament, you will be surprised at how many stories relate to today. God's command to Moses and the Israelites to go into the Promised Land and possess it is the fulfillment of a promise to Abraham that God made long before Moses was even born. It shows that God has a plan for history and that he keeps his promises.

It is essential for you, as a Christian, to realize that your heavenly Father keeps his promises! We are able to give him control of our lives because for centuries he has proven himself trustworthy. (See

86

Hebrews 11 for a brief recap of God's faithfulness.)

The Old Testament tells us about the real-life struggles people experienced when faced with the choice between trusting God and doing things their own way.

Instead of giving us all of history to read, God condensed his story in one book. He has even pointed out the most important lessons we need to pay attention to in order to live life to the fullest as his children.

Solomon, my son, get to know the God of your fathers. Worship and serve him with a clean heart and a willing mind, for the Lord sees every heart and understands and knows every thought. If you seek him, you will find him; but if you forsake him, he will permanently throw you aside. 1 Chronicles 28:9

I've grown up in a Christian family and believed in God all my life. But, recently I realized that I have been living off the faith of my parents. How do I have a faith that's mine?

This may be the most significant realization of your life. Some young people never understand that God wants us to know him personally. Living off of someone else's faith is like borrowing something from a friend. Whether you borrow a bike, clothes, skateboard, or tapes, it isn't yours and must be returned.

Solomon was challenged to get to know the "God of your fathers." In other words, he shouldn't settle for hearing how someone else trusted God. He should get to know him for himself.

During these years, your faith will be tested. Friends who don't believe in Christ may see nothing wrong with doing things that would cause your conscience to start screaming in your ear. That's when you'll have to make a choice—do I go along with my friends or do I stand on what I believe?

If *your* faith is strong—instead of being borrowed from your parents or your youth leader—no pressure from friends will be able to blow you away (Matthew 7:21-29).

Consider taking these steps to help you develop your faith.

First, make sure you have asked Jesus Christ to forgive your sin and come into your life. This is the first step to a personal relationship with God.

Second, begin to ask questions about the Bible. God wants you to *understand* it as well as *believe* and *obey* it. God is not afraid of honest questions asked with good motives.

Third, look for other Christians who are excited about developing their faith in God—people who don't want to settle for second best.

Being around growing Christians is contagious. What you learn from them will convince you that being a Christian is worth the work and is 100 percent right *for you!*

Early the next morning the army of Judah went out into the wilderness of Tekoa. On the way Jehoshaphat stopped and called them to attention. "Listen to me, O people of Judah and Jerusalem," he said. "Believe in the Lord your God, and you shall have success! Believe his prophets, and everything will be all right!"

After consultation with the leaders of the people, he determined that there should be a choir leading the march, clothed in sanctified garments and singing the song "His Loving-kindness Is Forever" as they walked along praising and thanking the Lord! And at the moment they began to sing and to praise, the Lord caused the armies of Ammon, Moab, and Mount Seir to begin fighting among themselves, and they destroyed each other! 2 Chronicles 20:20-22

I like the people in my church, but sometimes the worship service seems boring and confusing. Are all of the songs, readings, and rituals necessary?

A family decided to get a new refrigerator, so they bought one that was the top of the line and filled it with groceries. It was Friday, and they had a trip out of town planned, so they left. When they returned on Sunday, they opened the refrigerator door and were overwhelmed by a terrible odor. All of the food had spoiled!

There had been no power failure, and the refrigerator wasn't broken. Instead, they had forgotten to plug it in! Their brand new appliance, stuffed with food, was useless (and smelly) without being plugged in to the power.

We need to be plugged in, too, and worship is one way to do this. In worship we recognize God as the one who is in control and who has the power to change our circumstances and lives.

Jehoshaphat discovered this fact very graphically as he sent the worshipers out with his army. As the worshipers were singing, God miraculously provided a victory.

Worship takes many forms. Most of the songs and readings come right from Scripture. If you concentrate on the meaning behind what is being sung or read, you'll see that the words communicate very important facts about God.

When we sing a song many times, we will memorize it easier. You can probably sing every word of your favorite popular songs. Music helps us remember, even if it isn't the style we like best.

Another purpose of worship is to encourage us to grow in our faith. With all of the negative influences around us we need to be filled with courage to go out to face the world. This courage can help us live the Christian life when it seems that there's a war going on around us.

Worship is also the time for us to praise God for who he is and to thank him for all he's done. And being in church with our brothers and sisters in Christ worshiping together is like a family reunion.

Ephesians 5:19 was written during a time when Christians were put in prison for their faith. It says, "Talk with each other much about the Lord, quoting psalms and hymns and singing sacred songs, making music in your hearts to the Lord." By doing what this verse talks about, they were able to encourage each other as they reminded themselves of the faithfulness, goodness, and strength of God.

Remember, too, that knowing what is right to do and then not doing it is sin. James 4:17

I feel guilty more often now that I'm a Christian. Sometimes the guilt comes on for just little stuff that I used to never give a second thought about. When do I need to ask God for forgiveness?

God's goal is not to overwhelm us with our sin so that we become discouraged. He knows when to point out sin in our lives.

Some people are basically pretty "good" people when they come to faith in Christ. They don't have many destructive habits to overcome, and their parents have tried to teach them right from wrong.

Others come with a lot of sin "baggage."

Although each person is unique, we're the same when it comes to our nature—we're sinners. In fact, we were born with a sin nature. This is called "original sin." And throughout our lives, we do all sorts of things that are wrong.

When we receive Christ as Savior, God declares us "not guilty." But this doesn't mean that we're perfect and don't sin anymore. We must daily deal with sin while we're still alive on earth. It's part of being human. Christians, like everyone, have two types of sin to deal with. Past sins and present sins.

As I said, when we become Christians, all of our past sins are wiped away. "He has removed our sins as far away from us as the east is from the west" (Psalm 103:12). That's a distance that can't be measured!

Ideally, having past sins removed should also take away our guilt feelings. We can put the past behind us. We're forgiven!

But what about present sins? One of the roles of the Holy Spirit is to remind us when we sin. He doesn't do this to condemn us, but to prompt us to confess our sin, forsake it, and move on. God has forgiven us for these present sins too. We confess them to him to keep the communication channels open and to keep the relationship close. So we should talk to God about our life, and confess, whenever we need to. And remember, sin isn't limited to doing what is wrong. It also includes not doing what's right.

The passage in James 4:17 is plain. "Remember, too, that knowing what is right to do and then not doing it is sin."

If we know it's right to help someone with his homework . . . stop the gossip at the lunch table . . . give our parents the whole truth, instead of only part of it . . . turn off the TV and spend time with God . . . and don't do it—we sin!

Let God do the convicting in your life, not others, and you'll be glad to confess your sins to him. He's eager to clear away the barriers between you and start fresh.

Do you think I have come to give peace to the earth? No! Rather, strife and division! From now on families will be split apart, three in favor of me, and two against—or perhaps the other way around. A father will decide one way about me; his son, the other; mother and daughter will disagree; and the decision of an honored mother-in-law will be spurned by her daughter-in-law.
Luke 12:51-53

My older brother is always making fun of my new faith. How do I get him to stop?

People ridicule what they don't understand or what they wish they had themselves. It's really tough, though, when it comes from someone in your own family.

Your best defense is a quiet offense. "Don't snap back at those who say unkind things about you. Instead, pray for God's help for them, for we are to be kind to others, and God will bless us for it" (1 Peter 3:9).

When anyone makes fun of your faith, hold your tongue, pray for the person, be kind to him or her, and then wait for God's blessing. This verse ends with a promise directly from God. Though it doesn't say when God will bless you, or how God will bless you, it promises that he will bless you.

Here are some steps to take when facing opposition for your faith. (See 1 Peter 3:13-15).

First, check your attitude. If you understand that God is allowing you to experience this for a reason, you'll be able to thank him for it. It means that he believes in you enough to allow you to be tested.

Second, quietly trust yourself to Christ. You trusted Christ to be Lord of your life; now allow him to be Lord over your circumstances. God is trying to develop your character.

Third, be real, and be ready to explain your faith when the opportunities arise. Admit your faults, and don't act like you're superior to or better than the other person. This may disarm him or her to the point where he or she will see that you're not a threat. Then you may be able to share about Christ.

Even doing all of this still may not relieve the tension. So, "Remember, if God wants you to suffer, it is better to suffer for doing good than for doing wrong!" (1 Peter 3:17).

*When Mary arrived where Jesus was, she fell down at his feet,
saying, "Sir, if you had been here, my brother would still be alive."*

*When Jesus saw her weeping and the Jewish leaders wailing
with her, he was moved with indignation and deeply troubled.
"Where is he buried?" he asked them.*

They told him, "Come and see." Tears came to Jesus' eyes.
John 11:32-35

**Bad things seem to happen all the time. Does God care
about what is happening to people in the world? If he does,
why doesn't he do something about it?**

There are bad things that happen, and then there are tragedies. At
some time in life everyone will experience both of these. Let's look
at "bad things" first.

The person who flunks a math test had something bad happen to
him. Did he learn that it's important to keep up with assignments and
study before a test? We would hope so.

A ten-year-old boy races out from behind a parked car and is
almost hit by a car. He's scared to death, realizing that he could have
been killed! Did he learn a lesson about not darting into the street?
He better have; he may not get another chance!

In each case the person probably was not happy about what
happened. But *each situation in life, good or bad, is a learning
experience.*

Does God care that we learn important lessons about studying and
safety? He cares very much!

Ask your folks about the five worst things that have happened to
them. Then ask what they learned from these bad experiences.
Finally, ask them if they were thankful that these occurred.

Going through tough times is bad only when you don't learn
something from them.

Now let's discuss tragedy.

Unfortunately, no one is immune to what we believe is the ultimate
tragedy—death. It's the timing of death (especially for those who die

96

young), and how awful it can be (like an innocent victim at the hands of a drunk driver), that makes us wonder if God really cares.

When Adam and Eve disobeyed God in the Garden of Eden, their punishment was separation from God. This incident also set in motion the life cycle, ending in death. But the good news is that Jesus Christ's death on the cross killed death! Not physical death, but spiritual death for all those who receive his gift of forgiveness.

The curse that Adam brought the human race was physical death. Since that time man has invented some pretty ugly ways to make death happen (nuclear bombs, lung cancer, AIDS, and many others).

God knows that spiritual death is far worse than physical death. That's why he focused his attention on taking care of the penalty for our sin—spiritual death! (Romans 6:23).

God also knows how tragedy can point us to him and his purposes. "And we know that all that happens to us is working for our good if we love God and are fitting into his plans" (Romans 8:28).

Although God is not in heaven pushing buttons to make people die young, he can use even that situation for good. And remember, whatever happens to you, God cares. He loves you and wants to work out his purposes in your life.

"Ask, and you will be given what you ask for. Seek, and you will find. Knock, and the door will be opened. For everyone who asks, receives. Anyone who seeks, finds. If only you will knock, the door will open." Matthew 7:7-8

For more than six months I've been praying that my dad would become a Christian. Why hasn't God answered my prayer?

You've certainly been persistent. And you're doing exactly what this passage is talking about. You're "asking, seeking, and knocking."

God answers our prayers in three different ways: yes, no, or wait. In our instant society, where everything happens when we want it, "wait" answers are not the ones we like to hear. Especially when it seems as if the prayer is not being answered. But maybe it is.

God, in his perfect wisdom, knows the perfect way to lead people to respond to his call, turn from their sin, and come into a right relationship with him. If we try to manipulate circumstances, apart from God's will, these people may say no instead of yes.

Perhaps there's no one in your dad's life right now who could help him grow. Maybe there are important questions still unanswered that would cause him to respond out of emotion rather than with his will. Perhaps there are hurts or misconceptions about God and the church that still need to be worked through before he can begin to examine God's love for him.

Whatever the reason, the best thing you can do is to keep praying for him. Also, ask a friend whose father is a Christian if his or her dad would be able to start a friendship with your dad.

Unfortunately, persisting in prayer will not always change a heart that is hard toward God. People have a will and can choose to say no to any openings God's love may try to create. Your only hope is to continue your persistent prayer. Never give up.

What can we ever say to such wonderful things as these? If God is on our side, who can ever be against us? Since he did not spare even his own Son for us but gave him up for us all, won't he also surely give us everything else?

Who dares accuse us whom God has chosen for his own? Will God? No! He is the one who has forgiven us and given us right standing with himself.

Who then will condemn us? Will Christ? No! For he is the one who died for us and came back to life again for us and is sitting at the place of highest honor next to God, pleading for us there in heaven.

Who then can ever keep Christ's love from us? When we have trouble or calamity, when we are hunted down or destroyed, is it because he doesn't love us anymore? And if we are hungry, or penniless, or in danger, or threatened with death, has God deserted us?

No, for the Scriptures tell us that for his sake we must be ready to face death at every moment of the day—we are like sheep awaiting slaughter; but despite all this, overwhelming victory is ours through Christ who loved us enough to die for us. For I am convinced that nothing can ever separate us from his love. Death can't, and life can't. The angels won't, and all the powers of hell itself cannot keep God's love away. Our fears for today, our worries about tomorrow, or where we are—high above the sky, or in the deepest ocean—nothing will ever be able to separate us from the love of God demonstrated by our Lord Jesus Christ when he died for us. Romans 8:31-39

I don't feel like a Christian anymore. What's wrong?

Of course, something may be wrong if you're feeling guilty because you've disobeyed God. If so, you should feel guilty! If that's the case, admit your sin, ask God for forgiveness, and reopen communication with him.

But at other times, you may be feeling "normal." You see, Christians experience the whole range of emotions. They're happy, sad, fearful, angry, lonely, excited, apprehensive, and so on. Whatever the reason for these feelings, Christians feel them all at one time or another. That's what it means to be human and to live in an imperfect world.

Fortunately, your relationship with God doesn't depend on how you feel. It's based on *facts,* not feelings. It's a fact that Jesus died for you and that he rose from the dead. It's a fact that you gave your life by faith to him. And it's a fact that you now bear the mark of ownership of the Holy Spirit (2 Corinthians 5:17), and it is yours regardless of how you now feel.

Some people think that Christians should always be happy and confident, but that doesn't match what God says in his Word. We are told to "share the sorrow" of those who are sad (Romans 12:15). And Jesus wept because of the unbelief he saw in people around him (John 11:35). Later, Jesus promised his disciples that on earth they would have "many trials and sorrows" (John 16:33).

The Christians in Rome underwent severe persecution—many were tortured and killed because they believed in Christ. Surely they were torn with grief and pain. And yet Paul wrote to them (and to us) that "nothing can ever separate us from [God's] love" (Romans 8:38).

Christians experience all sorts of circumstances, struggles, and emotions. But the fantastic news is that no matter where we are, what we're facing, or what we're feeling, God is with us, and we can never be lost to his love.

"Yet there is one thing wrong; you don't love me as at first!"
Revelation 2:4

Because of my shyness and my family situation, I find it difficult to let people get close to me. As a Christian, I hear all the time how much God loves me. How close does God want to get with me?

As close as you'll let him.

God knows everything about us, and yet he still wants to be a Father to us. Isn't that amazing? King David wrote about how close God wants to be.

"How precious it is, Lord, to realize that you are thinking about me constantly! I can't even count how many times a day your thoughts turn towards me. And when I waken in the morning, you are still thinking of me!" (Psalm 139:17-18).

Knowing how much God thinks about us considering how little we think about him should give us an incredible feeling of worth. Our response to God's constant attentiveness, however, should never be out of obligation. God does not want us to come close to him only because we feel we have to.

This verse in Revelation warns us not to allow our love for God to grow weaker. God wants us to progress and grow beyond our initial commitment to him, just like in a marriage, where love should continue to grow. Unfortunately, this doesn't always happen. Many people who become Christians are really excited about their new relationship with God. But as problems come up, the excitement often wears off (just like what happens in some marriages).

To maintain a growing relationship with God, the key is time: daily time with him, time with others who know him, and time (in years) to grow to appreciate his love for you.

Though God is anxious for an intimate relationship with us, he'll wait for the day when we'll experience for ourselves what loving him really means.

O Timothy, you are God's man. Run from all these evil things, and work instead at what is right and good, learning to trust him and love others, and to be patient and gentle. Fight on for God. Hold tightly to the eternal life which God has given you, and which you have confessed with such a ringing confession before many witnesses. 1 Timothy 6:11-12

Trying to stay pure and not sin seems like a full-time job. How can anyone stay pure? Why would anyone want to?

Jesus talked a lot about the "Pharisees." These men had created long lists of dos and don'ts about behavior of every kind. They wanted to be pure! Many of them were very, very good.

But in Matthew 5:20 Jesus made an incredible statement! "I warn you—unless your goodness is greater than that of the Pharisees and other Jewish leaders, you can't get into the Kingdom of Heaven at all!"

Wow! If the Pharisees couldn't make it, then who can?

Those who make it into the kingdom of heaven are not just pure on the outside, like the Pharisees. Everyone can make sure their behavior is correct (at least for a while).

Jesus was talking about being pure on the inside. This begins with our accepting Christ's death on the cross as punishment for our sins. When we do this, we take on Christ's goodness, and, in God's eyes, we are pure and worthy of eternity in heaven! Now that's a pretty good deal!

It doesn't stop there, of course. God wants us to be like Jesus. This is a lifetime process of allowing God to mold us and change us. We do it by staying close to Christ and living like he wants us to. It's what keeps the Christian life fun, interesting, and challenging.

A Christian who's really alive realizes that his eternity is settled. But he also genuinely wants to be more like the one who paid such a high price for his soul—Jesus. His motivation is not to parade his goodness in front of others, but rather to please God.

Staying pure and growing as a Christian are "full-time jobs." But they are also natural by-products of staying close to Christ.

We can make our plans, but the final outcome is in God's hands.
Proverbs 16:1

I hear Christians talk a lot about God's will. Has God planned out everything I'll ever do?

Follow these instructions: Put your right hand straight up in the air. Next place your index finger in your left ear (come on, your left ear). Now clap your hands.

Who controlled your hand and fingers?

Tough question. Especially if you were silly enough to do what was asked. But we know from experience that people give us instructions, and we choose either to obey or not.

The question, however, is who has control—you or God? This has been debated for centuries, and the discussion can get quite complicated. For now, let's keep it as simple as possible.

We each have a will. There is a part within our brains that is the "chooser." Because we are human, the things we do don't often match up with what God wants us to do. It isn't God's will for us to sin.

Of course, God is strong enough to force his will on us. But because he loves us, he allows us to have choices. What loving, earthly father would force his child to say, "I love you, Daddy." Now, there would be no satisfaction in it at all.

God doesn't force us to follow him. And it is obvious that many use their will to reject Christ. In essence, they choose to go to hell!

Putting all of these facts together points to the conclusion that God has allowed our will to sometimes go against his will. One of the highest acts of love you can give someone is the opportunity to reject you. This is exactly what God has done.

So what is God's will for us?

First, it's to know him. "And this is the way to have eternal life—by knowing you, the only true God, and Jesus Christ, the one you sent to earth!" (John 17:3).

Second, it's to help others. "It is God himself who has made us what we are and given us new lives from Christ Jesus; and long ages ago he planned that we should spend these lives in helping others" (Ephesians 2:10).

Third, it's to be filled with the Holy Spirit. "So be careful how you act; these are difficult days. Don't be fools; be wise: make the most of every opportunity you have for doing good. Don't act thoughtlessly, but try to find out and do whatever the Lord wants you to. Don't drink too much wine, for many evils lie along that path; be filled instead with the Holy Spirit, and controlled by him" (Ephesians 5:15-18).

By allowing God to fill you, you are really saying, "God, take my will and help me do what you want."

You love him even though you have never seen him; though not seeing him, you trust him; and even now you are happy with the inexpressible joy that comes from heaven itself. And your further reward for trusting him will be the salvation of your souls.
1 Peter 1:8-9

It's hard to believe in anything you can't see. Why has God made it so difficult for people who would believe in him if they could only see him?

God is big, strong, powerful, and able to appear to anyone he wants. But if he did that, most people would feel forced or intimidated into following his orders rather than loved into following his example. God wants us to respond out of love for him, not fear!

The truth is that people *can* see God—through the eyes of faith. This means taking God at his Word—opening ourselves up to him. Some people say "seeing is believing." The truth is that "believing is seeing."

All of us believe in things we've never seen. A person in history. Gravity. The wind. Everyone has the ability to believe things that aren't seen. The bottom line for most who say, "I can't believe in something I haven't seen," is "I won't believe in God, because I want to run my own life." God doesn't work that way. Each person must trust in Christ, acknowledging him as Savior.

Beyond salvation, how does faith help the Christian?

"What is faith? It is the confident assurance that something we want is going to happen. It is the certainty that what we hope for is waiting for us, even though we cannot see it up ahead" (Hebrews 11:1).

God has not promised to show us the road ahead. He has only promised to walk with us as we go. Faith is a daily choice to believe in God's love, his promises, his presence, and his provision for our needs.

We want peace, direction, purpose, and love—God wants to give this, and more, to those who have faith.

106

Jesus said, "Blessed are those who haven't seen me and believe anyway" (John 20:29).

Don't be teamed with those who do not love the Lord, for what do the people of God have in common with the people of sin? How can light live with darkness? 2 Corinthians 6:14

I've been a Christian about nine months. Although I've made a lot of friends who are Christians, I still have quite a few who aren't. Should I still be hanging out with those friends who aren't Christians?

Find a quarter and two pennies. Place the quarter on a table. Put the two pennies about five inches below the quarter, one inch apart.

Now, pretend God is the quarter, you are the penny on the left, and your friend is the penny on the right. As you grow closer to God (move your penny up an inch or two), what happens to the distance between you and your friend? It gets wider! When only one person in a friendship moves closer to God, that's what happens to the relationship automatically.

There are degrees in friendships and stages we go through to make them stronger. But all friendships take time. And our closest friends affect us.

Think about the friends you used to hang around with. You probably did the same things, used the same slang, laughed at the same type of jokes, etc.

Hanging around with old friends who aren't Christians will probably not help you become a stronger Christian. That's what this verse is about. If you spend all of your deeper friendship time with unbelievers, you'll tend to stay like them and not move closer to God.

God doesn't want you to be totally isolated from those who aren't Christians. In fact, if you get to the point where you don't have any non-Christian friends, you're probably doing something wrong. If you're going to be Christ's representative to those who don't know him (see 2 Corinthians 5:18-20), you have to be around them! Just be careful, and remember that your goal is to point them to Christ.

"Be with wise men and become wise. Be with evil men and become evil" (Proverbs 13:20). And, "If you are looking for advice, stay away from fools" (Proverbs 14:7).

Especially in the early stages of your Christian life, you need to be around people who'll be your friends and also help you grow spiritually.

Then some of the elders of Israel visited me, to ask me for a message from the Lord, and this is the message that came to me to give to them:

"Son of dust, these men worship idols in their hearts—should I let them ask me anything? Tell them, the Lord God says: I the Lord will personally deal with anyone in Israel who worships idols and then comes to ask my help. For I will punish the minds and hearts of those who turn from me to idols." Ezekiel 14:1-5

It doesn't seem like I'm making too much progress as a Christian. It even seems like I'm going backwards. What can I do to reverse my reversal?

Until about age twenty-five, we grow physically. After twenty-five, we start to die. Fortunately, it usually takes another forty to fifty years before the dying process is complete!

Relationships can go through a living and dying process too. Our spiritual life is either living and growing, or it's in the process of dying. There is no such thing as leveling out or "plateauing."

You've hit the first stage of beginning to grow spiritually again. You recognize that you've been dying.

The second stage is discovering what caused the dying process. God confronted his people continually about this issue. Speaking through Ezekiel, he pinpointed the problem as idols that had replaced God in their hearts. That is, they had placed their affections on other things instead of God.

What has been pushing God out of your life? Is it TV, a friendship, sports, a boyfriend or girlfriend, music, fun? That's an idol and must be removed from the center of your life. After recognizing what has caused your heart to be drawn away from God, the next step is absolutely necessary. Turn around! This means confessing the problem to God and turning it over to his control (see 1 John 1:9).

God wants us to admit we've gone astray and then get on with maintaining a steady growth with him.

The third stage is the one that many Christians forget—finding

110

someone to hold us accountable. This person should encourage us, ask the tough questions, kick us in the pants when we need it, and pray for us often. We need someone who'll take the challenge of helping to guard our souls. The Bible calls this person a "shepherd."

This could be a friend your own age who has a real desire to grow spiritually. It could be a Christian adult whom you like and respect (parent, teacher, youth pastor, or someone from church). He or she can be anyone who is genuinely concerned for you, who won't get down on you, and who will always pull for you.

Ask God to send you such a person. This may be scary at first, but Christians who are consistently growing in their faith have learned the secret of giving others permission to help them stay on track. As long as you live, seek out someone who will walk with you. It will keep you from falling and provide you with close, lifelong friends.

But when you follow your own wrong inclinations, your lives will produce these evil results: impure thoughts, eagerness for lustful pleasure, idolatry, spiritism (that is, encouraging the activity of demons), hatred and fighting, jealousy and anger, constant effort to get the best for yourself, complaints and criticisms, the feeling that everyone else is wrong except those in your own little group—and there will be wrong doctrine. Galatians 5:19-20

I know that taking drugs is wrong, but I've asked my friends and they say the Bible doesn't talk about them. What should I say to someone if they ask me about drugs?

There are some areas where the Bible is silent. A good example is R-rated movies. Nowhere does the Bible specifically forbid attending movies that contain vulgar language, violence, or sex. In these cases, it's essential to seek the wisdom of those who know God's Word well. By looking at a number of passages, it's obvious an argument can be made about avoiding such movies.

Of course, there are many areas where the Bible is specific in its warnings. Homosexuality is a good example (see 1 Corinthians 6:9-10).

Then there are areas that are "hidden" to a degree. Taking drugs falls into this category.

Originally the New Testament was written in Greek, a much more complicated language than English. Trying to translate a word from Greek to English often requires a phrase.

The word *spiritism* that is, encouraging the activity of demons actually comes from the Greek noun *pharmakeia,* from which we get the word *pharmacy* better known as a drugstore!. When the Bible was translated, drug problems were not common, but there was "spiritism." So that's how the word *pharmakeia* was most often translated.

The connection is very frightening. Spiritism (sorcery, witchcraft) actually happens when drugs are taken! These aren't the aspirin type of drugs, but the kinds that alter a person's emotions, reflexes, and brain waves.

To get more specific, taking drugs is like opening your subconscious to demons! The connection between drugs and witchcraft is easily seen by going to the original Greek word.

Unknowingly, a person who takes drugs opens himself or herself to demonic influence. It's like an invitation to the spirit world to start influencing that person's life. That's why it's so dangerous. Most people aren't aware of this and have no idea what they're doing.

Although many may laugh at this explanation, it's a message that must be given to those who are taking drugs.

Drugs should also be avoided because they harm our bodies. The Bible is very clear about our responsibility to take care of ourselves. See 1 Corinthians 6:19-20; Romans 12:1-2; and 3 John 1:2-3.

That man is a fool who says to himself, "There is no God!" Anyone who talks like that is warped and evil and cannot really be a good person at all.

The Lord looks down from heaven on all mankind to see if there are any who are wise, who want to please God. But no, all have strayed away; all are rotten with sin. Not one is good, not one! Psalm 14:1-3

My dad says that since he's never hurt anyone, he's good enough to make it into heaven. I'm starting to agree with him. God won't send people who live good lives to hell, will he?

Teachers have developed two systems for grading their students' performance. First, there is the "curve." Put simply, 50 percent of a particular class will score above the average, 50 percent will score below. Often those who score below the average still have the chance to pass. That's why students seem to like this system best.

Then there is the set scale. With this system, a certain percentage determines your grade. If you get below 75 percent, for example, you fail.

Most people would like to believe that God grades on a curve. In other words, if they're better than others, it will be all right with God. All they have to do to pass is not kill anyone, not steal, mind their own business, and wait for heaven.

Unfortunately, God doesn't grade that way.

The passage you just read is clear. There isn't anyone who is good. Not one! All of us have strayed away. This doesn't mean we're all murderers. It means our heart is stained with the sin of Adam—the desire to be god in our life and run it ourselves. No one has a pure heart (see Luke 18:18-26 for a great illustration).

God is clear on *one* method of salvation. In his wisdom, he gave everyone the opportunity to go to heaven—by faith, not works. All a person has to do is believe that Christ paid the penalty for sin and rose again from the dead.

"Because of his kindness you have been saved through trusting Christ. And even trusting is not of yourselves; it too is a gift from God. Salvation is not a reward for the good we have done, so none of us can take any credit for it" (Ephesians 2:8-9).

Most people say this is too simple. But that's the whole idea! God isn't trying to make it tough on us. He wants us to be with him forever!

Throughout your life you'll run into people who believe that simply living a good life means heaven awaits. A good life is important to point people to a holy God, but it will not buy you a ticket to heaven. That ticket has already been paid by Jesus Christ.

Abel became a shepherd, while Cain was a farmer. At harvesttime Cain brought the Lord a gift of his farm produce, and Abel brought the fatty cuts of meat from his best lambs, and presented them to the Lord. And the Lord accepted Abel's offering, but not Cain's. This made Cain both dejected and very angry, and his face grew dark with fury. "Why are you angry?" the Lord asked him. "Why is your face so dark with rage?" Genesis 4:2-6

What does God really expect from me? I hear so much from so many people that I almost feel overwhelmed. I feel like I have to give up a lot in order to make God happy.

One essential quality of God is that he's very personal with *each* Christian. Although he chooses not to treat everyone alike, he does have expectations of his kids.

Some Christians may tell you about God's expectations based on where they are in their walk with him. If too many people are giving you advice, it could seem as though God expects way too much. This doesn't mean that you should quit listening to sincere Christians who want to help. It does mean however that if you're feeling overwhelmed, you're probably listening too much to others and not enough to God.

So what do you do? How *do you* please God?

The example from this story of Cain and Abel gives a significant piece to the puzzle. Each of these men brought something to God, but only Abel's sacrifice pleased him. One reason was that Cain's heart was not really in it. He tried to please God out of obligation instead of love.

The first key to pleasing God is found in our heart or our motivation. Do we really want to make God happy, or are we going through the motions because someone told us we should?

The second key to pleasing God is obedience: "The one who obeys me is the one who loves me; and because he loves me, my Father will love him; and I will too, and I will reveal myself to him" (John 14:21).

Good parents want their children to obey them in the essentials of how to live, how to avoid situations that will lead to pain or scars, and how to treat other people.

God is no different. But he's the perfect Father. He doesn't overload us with too many rules because he knows we would get discouraged.

Obedience to God is loving him enough to listen to what he says, then following through on what we know he is telling us.

This is why reading the Bible every day is so important. We cannot obey what we don't know. All that God wants us to know is written very plainly in his Word.

Through the Holy Spirit, God speaks to us as we come to him with willing hearts. He gently shows us areas in our lives that we need to examine and change according to his timetable, not someone else's.

The Jewish leaders were stung to fury by Stephen's accusation and ground their teeth in rage. But Stephen, full of the Holy Spirit, gazed steadily upward into heaven and saw the glory of God and Jesus standing at God's right hand. And he told them, "Look, I see the heavens opened and Jesus the Messiah standing beside God, at his right hand!"

Then they mobbed him, putting their hands over their ears, and drowning out his voice with their shouts, and dragged him out of the city to stone him. The official witnesses—the executioners—took off their coats and laid them at the feet of a young man named Paul.

And as the murderous stones came hurtling at him, Stephen prayed, "Lord Jesus, receive my spirit." And he fell to his knees, shouting, "Lord, don't charge them with this sin!" and with that, he died. Acts 7:54-60

Some kids at school (and even some teachers) give Christians a pretty tough time. This makes me not want to let anyone know I'm a believer. What should I do?

Rejection comes with being a Christian because our lives and beliefs go against the flow of the rest of the world. Growing closer to God will naturally make you grow farther away from the world.

Stephen took a stand for Christ that cost him much more than rejection from a few friends. It cost him his life.

As you read further in Acts 8 and 9, you'll see what the results of a fearless faith can be.

Imagine being able to see all of history from beginning to end. You would understand so much more because you could see the whole picture.

Only God can do that—so we have to trust him. We have to live on this earth without being able to see the future.

If Stephen had known what his death would accomplish, he would have died smiling.

A man named Paul was one of the foremost persecutors of

Christians. But Paul's life was turned around, and he became a follower of Christ. Paul had heard Stephen and had watched him die.

Paul didn't just become a church-only, pew-sitter type of follower. He traveled throughout the world, sharing the Good News about Christ. He also wrote nearly half of the New Testament! Stephen's rejection helped bring Paul to Christ.

People are watching you and other Christians at school. They are seeing how you respond to rejection and verbal abuse. Within those crowded halls are people who want to believe in something true, something worth living for, no matter what the cost. And when they find it, they may make an incredible impact in their world for Christ.

What do they learn from watching you?

That's a good question, why don't we let our sweet little miss holier-than-thou "Christian" answer it!

"Don't imagine that I came to bring peace to the earth! No, rather, a sword. I have come to set a man against his father, and a daughter against her mother, and a daughter-in-law against her mother-in-law—a man's worst enemies will be right in his own home! If you love your father and mother more than you love me, you are not worthy of being mine; or if you love your son or daughter more than me, you are not worthy of being mine. If you refuse to take up your cross and follow me, you are not worthy of being mine.

"If you cling to your life, you will lose it; but if you give it up for me, you will save it." Matthew 10:34-39

My parents are quietly putting up with my new faith. Mom thinks it's "nice" and Dad won't talk to me about it. How do I make them see Jesus is a real person?

There are many difficult sayings of Jesus in the New Testament. This is one of the toughest. What does Jesus mean when he says "a man's worst enemies will be right in his own home"?

If you've faced pressure and opposition from friends because of your new faith, you realize that your decision for Christ causes people to make decisions *about you*. Some will stay with you and support your decision because they are your true friends. Others will leave because they don't understand. Some will simply quit calling because your values no longer encourage their life-style.

We may also find opposition at home. In these verses, Jesus isn't telling us to be disobedient to our parents or to try to cause problems at home. He's just stating the fact that a person with different goals, values, purposes, perhaps even morals, may cause division. More than a fact, it's a promise! Rarely will the only Christian in a household go unchallenged.

Though it's uncommon for parents to be openly hostile toward someone in their home, it does happen. Put-downs can really hurt, especially if they come from someone you love.

The best course of action is to not try to make your parents see anything. Instead, just live your life in obedience to them as the Bible commands.

"Children, obey your parents; this is the right thing to do because God has placed them in authority over you. Honor your father and mother. This is the first of God's Ten Commandments that ends with a promise. And this is the promise: that if you honor your father and mother, yours will be a long life, full of blessing" (Ephesians 6:1-3).

It's not your role to make them change. That's the job of the Holy Spirit. "And when he has come he will convince the world of its sin, and of the availability of God's goodness, and of deliverance from judgment" (John 16:8). You are to be God's representative in your home, hopefully to bring your family to Christ.

Don't neglect your family because they don't yet accept your faith. But don't neglect the higher mission of keeping God as your number one priority either.

Find some Christian friends who will pray *for you* and pray *with you* about your situation. Go to them for encouragement and advice when you face each difficult situation.

For in those days Israel had no king, so everyone did whatever he wanted to—whatever seemed right in his own eyes.
Judges 17:6

A friend says that my new faith in Christ is too narrow because Christians believe Christ is the only way to God. Why can't God accept different ideas by other religions?

Suppose your history teacher told you that Columbus discovered America in 1492. Just then, four other people raised their hands and said, "I think he discovered America in 1454 (or 1678 or 1543 or 1733). What makes you the authority on history anyway? We are going to believe what we think is right."

Do these kids have the freedom to believe what they think is right? Of course they do.

A wise teacher would likely respond, "You may believe any date you choose to believe, but there is only one right answer and I have told you what it is. If you put a different answer on the test at the end of the term, it will be marked wrong."

God has given people the freedom to choose what they want to believe about who he is and what his plan is for human beings. But when the test scores are graded at the end of the age, there will be only one right answer.

During this period in Jewish history they had no leader, so it says that "everyone did whatever he wanted to—whatever seemed right in his own eyes." What this means is that not only did people choose to disobey God as their leader, but their actions were evil as well. Throughout history people have behaved according to what they believed about God.

If people believe that God doesn't exist or that God doesn't care how we live and treat each other, they will likely act accordingly. Usually, this means that they treat themselves or others like there will be no final exam when they pass on to the next life!

Jesus said, "I am the Way—yes, and the Truth and the Life. No one can get to the Father except by means of me" (John 14:6). This means that God grades on a pass/fail basis depending on what we have done with his Son, Jesus.

God has given people the freedom to believe any "religion" they want. But the final authority is not their own beliefs. There is only one right answer. God's standard is faith in Jesus Christ, his death on the cross, and his resurrection so that our sin would not eternally separate us from God.

Then again, this may be too "narrow". Perhaps we should say that the answer is "somewhere in the early thirties"

Young man, it's wonderful to be young! Enjoy every minute of it! Do all you want to; take in everything, but realize that you must account to God for everything you do. So banish grief and pain, but remember that youth, with a whole life before it, can make serious mistakes. Don't let the excitement of being young cause you to forget about your Creator. Honor him in your youth before the evil years come—when you'll no longer enjoy living. It will be too late then to try to remember him when the sun and light and moon and stars are dim to your old eyes, and there is no silver lining left among your clouds. For there will come a time when your limbs will tremble with age, your strong legs will become weak, and your teeth will be too few to do their work, and there will be blindness too. Then let your lips be tightly closed while eating when your teeth are gone! And you will waken at dawn with the first note of the birds; but you yourself will be deaf and tuneless, with quavering voice. You will be afraid of heights and of falling—a white-haired, withered old man, dragging himself along: without sexual desire, standing at death's door, and nearing his everlasting home as the mourners go along the streets.

Yes, remember your Creator now while you are young— before the silver cord of life snaps and the gold bowl is broken; before the pitcher is broken at the fountain and the wheel is broken at the cistern; then the dust returns to the earth as it was, and the spirit returns to God who gave it. All is futile, says the Preacher; utterly futile. Ecclesiastes 11:9–12:8

Although I recently became a Christian, I'm having second thoughts. I feel like I'll miss out on a lot of fun during my teenage years. Can't I wait until later to live for Christ?

A speaker once told of having a dream. The location was hell, and the demons were trying to think of ways to stop people from accepting Christ.

Each demon brought an idea to Satan and was given approval to try it. The ideas included the typical ones people often think are responsible for turning others away: drugs, sexual temptations, intellectualism, money, fame, and status.

All of these strategies were tried by various demons, and they weren't very effective.

Finally, one demon suggested a plan that surprised everyone. He said they should tell people that believing the Bible and following Christ were the right things to do; and to tell them that being a committed believer was the only way to live life. "But," he concluded, "tell them to do it—*tomorrow!*"

That has become Satan's strategy. And for many people tomorrow never comes!

This delaying tactic works like Novocain. It numbs people and keeps them from turning to the truth when they hear it.

We are creatures of habit. Almost everything we know we learned by repetition—reading, writing, math, speech, and manners—have all been learned by doing the same thing over and over again.

Our thoughts about God are the same way. If when we're young we believe that we can play now and get committed later, we fulfill Satan's strategy.

Thought patterns become habits; habits become beliefs; beliefs become actions; and actions determine our eternity!

You may feel like you'll miss out on the fun, but the "good times" don't last. Most of what the world pursues is shallow and meaningless (though sometimes "fun," for a while).

To live life to the fullest, we need to follow God, not in fear that he wants to take away our fun, but in faith that he wants to make our lives into something we can be proud of.

Life begins for people the moment they realize that the world doesn't revolve around *them*, but around God who made the world and all that is in it.

The heart is the most deceitful thing there is and desperately wicked. No one can really know how bad it is! Only the Lord knows! He searches all hearts and examines deepest motives so he can give to each person his right reward, according to his deeds—how he has lived. Jeremiah 17:9-10

I've done some pretty awful things in my life—things that other kids never even think about doing. I really don't see how God could forgive me for what I've done.

Recognizing that you've done wrong is 90 percent of the battle.

Usually, people who build up years of wrong actions have also built a shell around their hearts. The shell protects them from feeling guilty about something they've done wrong. As the shell gets harder and thicker, they continue the downward spiral, doing more and more things that are wrong.

Jeremiah, a prophet of God, looked at the human tendency to sin and came to this conclusion: "The heart is the most deceitful thing there is, and desperately wicked." As you'll notice, it doesn't say that some people's hearts are more wicked than others. All of us have the potential for actions that destroy ourselves and others.

We can be glad God has chosen not to leave us this way. We would all be without hope if it weren't for God's grace. God says in Isaiah 43:25, "I, yes, I alone am he who blots away your sins for my own sake and will never think of them again."

Whatever you've done, God isn't surprised and will forgive you if you let him.

Your own recognition of wrong is the first step. God has opened up your heart so you can take a look at its ugliness. Now you must make a decision whether you want to leave it that way or allow him to come in and clean it up.

"Come, let's talk this over! says the Lord; no matter how deep the stain of your sins, I can take it out and make you as clean as freshly fallen snow. Even if you are stained as red as crimson, I can make you white as wool!" (Isaiah 1:18).

126

Don't give up—give in . . . to God. Ask him to forgive you and help you start over.

im sorry God, but i'm afraid i'm just too bad for you to clean.

The Lord says, "The people of Israel have sinned again and again, and I will not forget it. I will not leave them unpunished any more. For they have perverted justice by accepting bribes and sold into slavery the poor who can't repay their debts; they trade them for a pair of shoes. They trample the poor in the dust and kick aside the meek. . . .

"Yet think of all I did for them! I cleared the land of the Amorites before them—the Amorites, as tall as cedar trees, and strong as oaks! But I lopped off their fruit and cut their roots. And I brought you out from Egypt and led you through the desert forty years, to possess the land of the Amorites. And I chose your sons to be Nazirites and prophets—can you deny this, Israel?" asks the Lord. "But you caused the Nazirites to sin by urging them to drink your wine, and you silenced my prophets, telling them, 'Shut up!'

"Therefore, I will make you groan as a wagon groans that is loaded with sheaves. Your swiftest warriors will stumble in flight. The strong will all be weak, and the great ones can no longer save themselves. The archer's aim will fail, the swiftest runners won't be fast enough to flee, and even the best of horsemen can't outrun the danger then. The most courageous of your mighty men will drop their weapons and run for their lives that day." The Lord God has spoken. Amos 2:6-16

My friends are always doing things that my conscience won't let me get away with, yet they never seem to get caught. Why does it seem like a lot of bad stuff never gets punished?

At the dentist, Novocain deadens the nerves in our mouth so we won't feel the pain of the drill. The conscience can also be numbed by repeated sin, so that the person no longer feels guilty about wrong behavior. Be glad that you have an active conscience. It means that you're still sensitive to sin. And remember, all sins have consequences.

Some wrong actions have immediate consequences. If someone

cheats on a test while the teacher is watching, the immediate consequence will be an *F.*

Other actions have short-term, delayed consequences. Some
people cheat on their income-tax returns. For a year or two, they
seem to get away with it. But eventually, the IRS audits their returns,
discovers the problems, and then levies a hefty fine or even sends
them to prison.

Still other actions seem to never get punished. The key word is
seem. The Bible is very clear about what will happen in the long run
to actions contrary to God's plan.

"Don't be misled; remember that you can't ignore God and get
away with it: a man will always reap just the kind of crop he sows! If
he sows to please his own wrong desires, he will be planting seeds
of evil and he will surely reap a harvest of spiritual decay and death;
but if he plants the good things of the Spirit, he will reap the
everlasting life which the Holy Spirit gives him" (Galatians 6:7-8).

If we "sow," or throw bad actions around, we'll reap the fruit of
that kind of seed.

The same is true when we sow things that are good. If we are
genuinely trying to follow close to God, reading our Bible, commu-
nicating with him, etc., God will use us, and we'll reap a wonderful
harvest.

It can get tiring, however, always trying to be good, especially
when there's so much bad around us. That's when we have to
remember God's promise of the eventual harvest.

"And let us not get tired of doing what is right, for after a while we
will reap a harvest of blessing if we don't get discouraged and give
up" (Galatians 6:9).

The prophet Amos told the people of Israel what would happen if
they didn't shape up. They were numb toward the things of God. They
even oppressed the poor, selling some into slavery. His predictions
didn't immediately come true. After many years, however, he proved
to be right. The Israelites were conquered by the Assyrians and were
made slaves, receiving exactly what they had given out.

If you didn't find the answers to your questions about growing in the Christian faith, please take the time to write:

Greg Johnson
c/o Tyndale House Publishers
P. O. Box 80
Wheaton, IL 60189

I'll do everything I can to get you a speedy reply.

Greg Johnson